insight text guide

Justine McGinnis

The Bone Sparrow

Zana Fraillon

First published in 2021, reprinted in 2023, 2024.

Insight Publications Pty Ltd
3/350 Charman Road
Cheltenham VIC 3192
Australia
Tel: +61 3 8571 4950
Email: books@insightpublications.com.au

www.insightpublications.com.au

A catalogue record for this book is available from the National Library of Australia

Zana Fraillon's The Bone Sparrow / Justine McGinnis

Justine McGinnis asserts the moral right to be identified as the author of this work.

ISBNs:
9781922525673 (print)
9781922525680 (digital)

Cover design by Gisela Beer

Printed by Markono Print Media Pte Ltd

contents

CHARACTER MAP

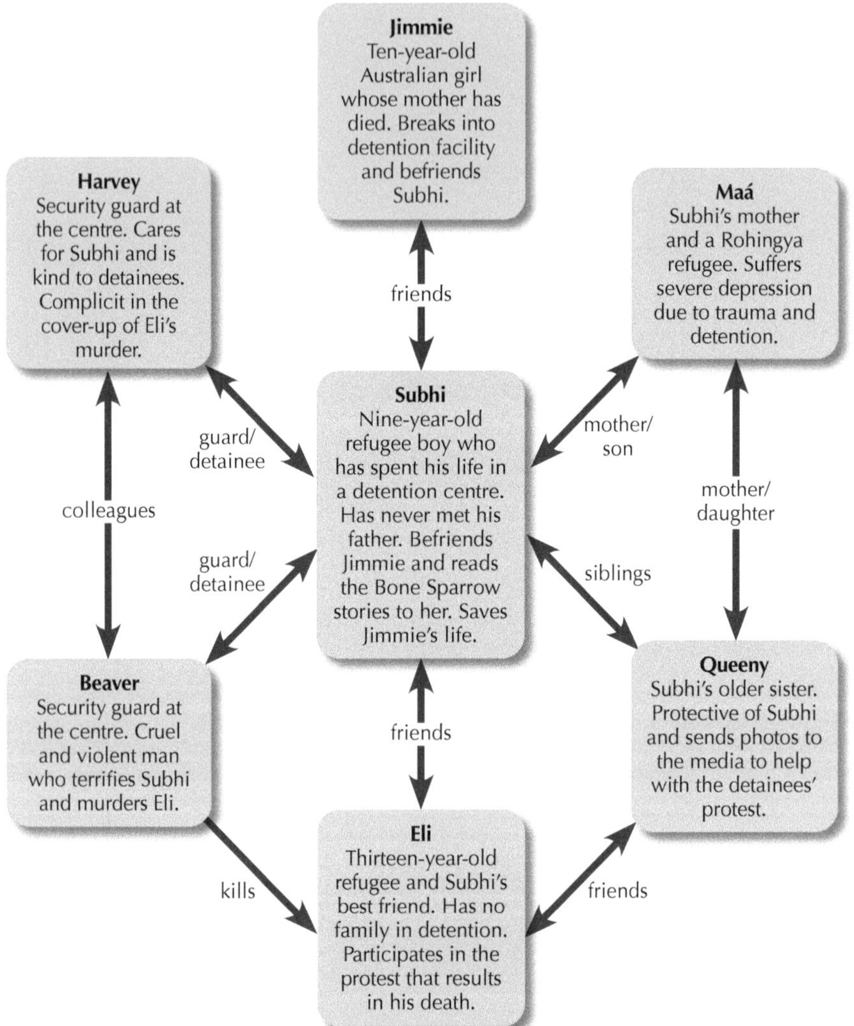

OVERVIEW

About the author

Zana Fraillon is an Australian author from Melbourne. With degrees in history and education, Fraillon worked as a primary school teacher before becoming an author. Her published work includes picture books, and novels for children and young adults.

The Bone Sparrow was published in 2016 and went on to win the 2017 ABIA Book of the Year for Older Children and the Readings Young Adult Book Prize.

Synopsis

Protagonist Subhi's life in the detention centre is bleak. His mother, Maá, is depressed and his sister, Queeny, has become hardened by deprivation and confinement. He imagines a Night Sea washing over the camp, bringing treasure from the father he has never met.

After hearing rumours about the refugees being given bicycles and wanting to know the truth, Jimmie breaks into the centre and meets Subhi. Desperate to hear the words in her mother's notebook, Jimmie returns to the centre so Subhi can read it to her. He begins to read the story of Anka, Oto and Iliya, and is frightened by Jimmie's Bone Sparrow necklace.

Subhi struggles after his friend Eli is moved to Alpha Compound and is jealous of Eli's secret conversations with Queeny and the Alpha men. He discovers Queeny is planning to send photographs of the detainees to the media and is terrified she will be caught, not understanding her desire to inform the world outside of conditions inside the centre.

Subhi is devastated when fellow detainee Nasir dies but is comforted by a visit from Jimmie. They read about soldiers capturing Anka, and Oto commencing a journey with the Bone Sparrow to find her. Subhi begins to wonder if perhaps the Bone Sparrow does bring protection.

There is dread in the air as detainees fall ill with food poisoning. Jimmie and Subhi read about Anka giving birth to a son and Oto's continuing journey. Maá's condition deteriorates.

The protest in Alpha begins and Queeny photographs Eli holding a banner over the men who have sewn their lips together. Jimmie sees Queeny's photograph in the newspaper and feels despondent about the conditions the refugees endure, so brings Subhi a feast. Returning home, she climbs into the attic to get her mother's belongings and cuts her arm on a piece of metal. She falls ill and is left alone when her father leaves for his final shift.

As tensions at the centre rise, Subhi buries the knife he found earlier. Jimmie visits but is feverish and disoriented. She leaves her book behind and collapses outside her house. On his own, Subhi reads the final Bone Sparrow story, in which Anka and Oto reunite. Subhi sees Jimmie's torch flashing the signal for help but cannot escape due to increased patrols and searchlights.

By morning, the protestors have barricaded themselves inside Alpha and the Jackets are preparing their riot gear. In the chaos Subhi escapes and finds Jimmie. He reads her the final Bone Sparrow story as they await an ambulance.

At the centre, a riot is raging and Subhi watches Eli scramble under a bush for the knife that Subhi has moved. Unable to defend himself, Eli is viciously assaulted by one of the guards, Beaver, while another guard, Harvey, watches in silence.

The Jackets cover up Eli's murder and Subhi is devasted by Harvey's complicity. Subhi is conflicted, knowing that if he speaks up, Harvey will be punished. The Night Sea comes and when Subhi sees Eli's whale, he knows he must tell Eli's story.

Maá wakes and Subhi finally hears her voice again. Queeny gives Subhi a book of their father Ba's poems, revealing she was behind the Night Sea treasures and that Ba died some time ago. Jimmie visits and gives Subhi the Bone Sparrow necklace. Investigators arrive and, as Subhi goes with the investigator Sarah to tell the truth about Eli's death, a tearful Harvey nods in support.

Subhi imagines the rest of Iliya's story – that he survived and fell in love with a Rohingya woman, entwining Jimmie's family's story with his own. Subhi feels brave about testifying, and he and Maá hear Eli's whale singing to the moon.

Character summaries

Subhi

A Rohingya refugee living with his mother and sister in an immigration detention facility. He is nine years old at the beginning of the novel; the birthday he celebrates is his tenth. Born in detention, Subhi has never met his father or known life outside the fences.

Jimmie

A ten-year-old Australian girl who lives with her father and brother near the detention facility. Jimmie is illiterate, lonely and grieving for her mother. She befriends Subhi when she sneaks into the detention centre.

Eli

A thirteen-year-old refugee who has lost his entire family. He is Subhi's best friend. He runs a covert package distribution business in the centre before being moved to Alpha, where he joins the protest that leads to the riots and his death.

Queeny

Subhi's sister, who is approximately twelve years old. She's forthright, bossy and hardened by life. She wants things to change and takes action by sending photographs to the media.

Maá

Subhi and Queeny's mother, and a Rohingya refugee. She is severely traumatised and grieving the death of her husband.

Harvey

A guard who looks out for Subhi and treats detainees with respect and kindness. However, he does not protest the cruelty of other guards.

Beaver

A vicious and ruthless guard who terrifies Subhi and murders Eli during the riot.

The Jackets

The security guards who control every aspect of the detainees' lives.

The Shakespeare duck

A rubber duck resembling William Shakespeare. He becomes Subhi's wisecracking imaginary friend, helping Subhi cope and voicing his subconscious.

Jonah

Jimmie's sixteen-year-old brother. He loves Jimmie and is responsible for her while their father is away, but often leaves her to fend for herself.

Jimmie's father

An Australian man who loves his children but struggles with grief following the death of his wife. His job takes him away for long periods.

Nasir

An elderly detainee who lives with Subhi's family and is like a grandfather to Subhi.

Sarah

An official investigating the riots.

BACKGROUND & CONTEXT

In an article for *The Guardian* Fraillon revealed that the inspiration for *The Bone Sparrow* was a drawing by a child in Australian immigration detention, depicting themselves trapped behind a fence, crying tears of blood as a hateful sun glares down on them. Constructing the narrative through Subhi's point of view allows Fraillon to capture the fear and injustice implicit in that picture.

Australian values

The Bone Sparrow endorses and appeals to many Australian values, while challenging and questioning others.

Australia's history of British colonisation has influenced national identity, with many social values harking back to the penal colony era and the experiences of early settlers, as well as those of the ANZACs. Values that persist today include:

- egalitarianism – a 'fair go' for all
- anti-authoritarianism – cynicism towards authorities
- mateship – fierce loyalty to one's close friends.

In the contemporary era, dominant Australian values also include:

- freedom
- democracy
- prosperity
- family and relationships
- multiculturalism and diversity
- equality and justice.

The Department of Home Affairs outlines Australia's democratic values, which are 'based on freedom, respect, fairness and equality of opportunity' (DHA 2021), and all refugee and humanitarian visa applicants are required to sign and agree to the Australian Values Statement. These values are outlined in detail on the department's website at https://www.homeaffairs.gov.au/about-us/our-portfolios/social-cohesion/australian-values.

Geographical context

The Bone Sparrow is set in regional Australia. While no specific location is identified, references to crocodiles and red-bellied black snakes allude to Far North Queensland. However, the detention centre embodies conditions of many such Australian facilities. Detainees live in tents and battle heat, mould and storms, reflecting the conditions of offshore facilities in Nauru and on Manus Island and Christmas Island. Likewise, characters endure isolation, a harsh climate and limited resources, typical of many current and past regional facilities.

Refugees and asylum seekers

The United Nations High Commissioner for Refugees (UNHCR) reported that in 2016 there were 65.6 million forcibly displaced people in the world. Of these, 22.5 million were refugees, with fifty-one per cent of this group being children, like Subhi, Queeny and Eli. It is important to understand the terms used to refer to people at various stages of the process of seeking asylum, especially as these terms are often misused in popular discourse. Some key definitions are given below.

Asylum seeker: any person seeking sanctuary outside their home country.

Forcibly displaced person: someone involuntarily fleeing their home nation due to war, persecution, human rights violations or natural disasters. All refugees have been forcibly displaced, but not all forcibly displaced people are refugees.

Illegal immigrant: a person residing in a country without a valid visa, such as tourists whose visas have expired. Refugees and asylum seekers are not illegal immigrants, despite the common misconception that they are. International law protects their right to cross international borders by any means, before or after lodging an asylum claim.

Migrant: a person who voluntarily chooses to move to another country.

Refugee: as defined by the 1951 Refugee Convention, someone who has crossed an international border to escape persecution due to religion, race, nationality, political opinion or membership of a particular social group.

Stateless person: someone not recognised as a legal citizen of any country.

International law

International treaties (also called conventions) are legally binding contracts. Many treaties are currently in effect, addressing concerns such as human rights, warfare, trade, environmental management and maritime relations. While international law is difficult to enforce, several bodies (such as the United Nations), tribunals and courts govern compliance. Failure to abide by international treaties can result in economic sanctions, criticism and damage to a state's reputation, and, in extreme cases, military action. The Universal Declaration of Human Rights outlines the rights and freedoms of all humans. Some articles relevant to *The Bone Sparrow* include these rights:

- to be free and equal
- not to suffer cruel or degrading treatment
- not to endure arbitrary arrest, detention or exile
- to seek and receive asylum from persecution
- to own personal property
- to have a standard of living adequate for health and wellbeing
- to receive an education.

The 1951 Refugee Convention outlines refugees' entitled protections and rights. Under this, refugees are permitted to cross borders in search of asylum and are protected regardless of whether they make a claim for asylum before or after entering a country. The law does not discriminate between means of arrival; the same rights apply whether a border has been crossed by plane, vehicle or boat. Other treaties that protect refugees include the Convention against Torture and Other Cruel, Inhuman or

Degrading Treatment or Punishment, and the Convention on the Rights of the Child. Australia is a signatory to all these agreements.

Australia's immigration policies

Currently, the Australian government grants 6000 protection visas per year to refugees, and those permanently settled constitute just three per cent of Australia's total migration intake (Karlson 2016). Since 1992, Australia has had a policy of **mandatory detention** in which non-citizens without a valid visa must be detained until a visa is granted or they leave the country. Since then, numerous other policies have been implemented to reduce boat arrivals, curtail people-smuggling operations and tighten border security. This includes the Pacific Solution (the policy of detaining asylum seekers on islands in the Pacific Ocean instead of in mainland Australia) and the *Australian Border Force Act 2015* (which initially prohibited immigration staff, including doctors and nurses, from disclosing 'protected information' regarding detention centres). A detailed timeline is available on the Refugee Council of Australia's website (see RCOA 2021, p.79). Some ways these policies are alluded to in the novel include the following:

- The Alpha men's transfer to an overseas transit centre refers to Australia's detention facilities on Manus Island and Nauru, which were first used for offshore processing as part of the Pacific Solution.
- The plan to send detainees in Alpha back to their home countries represents the Rudd government's policy of refusing resettlement to all boat arrivals.
- Detainee Ishan's mention of abuse by both civilians and police at the Transit Centre is a reference to Nauru's open detention program.
- Nasir living in permanent detention despite his verified refugee claim, due to an adverse risk assessment, refers to adverse security assessments that can be issued by the Australian Security Intelligence Organisation (ASIO). Nasir never learns why he is a risk because ASIO is not required to provide a written statement to detained people.

Australia's immigration policies have been accused of breaching international conventions such as the 1951 Refugee Convention, the Universal Declaration of Human Rights, the International Covenant on Civil and Political Rights, and the Convention on the Rights of the Child. Critics include the United Nations, Amnesty International, the Australian Human Rights Commission, the Law Council of Australia, the Australian Psychological Society, academics and human rights experts. Common concerns, many of which are addressed in the novel, include:

- the imprisonment of children
- asylum seekers being subjected to inhumane conditions and abuse
- asylum seekers having limited access to medical care, legal services and education
- asylum seekers lacking access to family reunification
- unreasonable processing times
- policies that discriminate against boat arrivals
- secrecy laws that threaten imprisonment for employees who disclose to the media or the public certain information they might become aware of, witness or hear while carrying out their work.

A 2012 parliamentary report found that detention had disastrous effects on adults and children, including:

- rates of depression, post-traumatic stress disorder, suicidal behaviour and self-harm significantly higher than the national average
- insomnia and mental decline
- exacerbation of previous trauma
- riots and violence resulting from desperation and mental illness (JSCAIDN 2012).

Hunger strikes and rioting

As depicted in the novel, desperation often leads to extreme methods of protest, with dozens of protests and riots in detention centres reported in the media over the past few decades. Human rights academic Lucy Fiske explains: 'Hunger strikes, lip sewing and self-harm [are] strategies used by detainees' to 'make visible the injustice of the state' given their treatment has been largely concealed from the public (Fiske 2016, p.142). When anger and powerlessness are amplified, detention centres become 'laboratory incubators for riots' (Fiske 2016, p.185).

Persecution of the Rohingya people

Subhi's family are members of the Rohingya people, an ethnic minority of Myanmar (formerly Burma), who have been called 'one of the most persecuted minorities in the world' (Young 2017). They have lived in northern Rakhine State since the eighth century and, as the largest of several Muslim minorities in the predominantly Buddhist nation, have endured a long history of persecution.

Burma became a republic in 1948 and at this time all citizens were afforded equal rights. A military coup in 1962 resulted in a new constitution and the start of a systematic campaign of state-sanctioned persecution of the Rohingya. Since then, they have been stripped of citizenship, denied human rights, and victimised by racism and hate speech. Laws have subjected adults and children to forced labour and have restricted their movement, ability to work and own property, and freedom to marry and bear children. Since the 1970s, military operations have enacted ethnic cleansing through deportation, mass arrests, rape, executions and the destruction of homes. In 1982, Burma implemented a Citizenship Law that effectively rendered the Rohingya people stateless and caused them to be officially considered 'aliens' in their own land, following their exclusion from a list of national races of Burma. Several hundred thousand Rohingya fled Myanmar in the decades prior to 2016.

Sadly, since the novel was published in 2016, the crisis has worsened. Brutal 'clearance operations' were launched by the government in 2016 and 2017, leading to more than 700 000 Rohingya fleeing the country by the end of 2017 (more than half the Rohingya population in Myanmar at the time). As this guide goes to press, the crisis is ongoing.

Rohingya culture and stories

Oral traditions are important to the Rohingya people. Many of Maá's 'Listen Now stories' were 'passed down from maás to their kids since forever back' (p.36) while Ba told Subhi stories 'through Maá's belly ... from a time so long gone that he couldn't know except by being told them himself' (p.35).

The value of storytelling to the cultural identity and survival of the Rohingya people is reflected in the novel. *Taranas* (Rohingya music and poetry) took on renewed value in the face of ethnic cleansing. The Myanmar government attempted to silence the Rohingya with laws prohibiting music and theatre, and people expressing their culture frequently face punishment, as when Ba is 'arrested for writing his poems' (p.36). As the Rohingya population has dispersed around the globe, *taranas* have become a vital way of preserving culture and identity.

Regional disadvantage

Jimmie's story reflects the reality that rural and remote regions of Australia suffer higher levels of disadvantage than urban areas. Examples include lower incomes and higher rates of unemployment; financial hardship and poverty; lower life expectancy; limited access to services such as health, education and transport; fewer people completing secondary school and higher rates of truancy; and higher rates of mental illness. The causes of this inequity are complex and the degree of hardship varies depending on the remoteness of an area and the unique circumstances of different communities. Contributing factors include isolation and distance; lack of government services; economic deregulation and government cost-cutting leading to school, hospital and bank closures; changes to industry that result in the closure of mines and factories; and declining towns and urbanisation.

GENRE, STRUCTURE & LANGUAGE

Genre

Children's fiction

The Bone Sparrow is a novel for older children and early teen readers. Features of children's fiction evident include a child protagonist and children learning to manage the world independently. The confronting subject matter is handled appropriately for the intended audience. For example, graphic imagery is omitted from the depiction of Eli's death and humour balances darker content.

Realistic fiction

The Bone Sparrow conforms to the conventions of realistic fiction. There is a strong focus on **verisimilitude** as characters, events and setting are credible. While there is an element of fantasy in the portrayal of the Night Sea, this does not challenge the verisimilitude, owing to Subhi's first-person narration. The Night Sea is a believable representation of childhood imagination – no one else sees it and the treasures that initially seem to appear magically are later revealed to have been left by Queeny.

Coming-of-age stories

Coming-of-age stories focus on a naive protagonist undergoing psychological and moral growth. There is usually a loss of innocence as the protagonist enters the adult world, and stories often involve a difficult journey of self-discovery. While such fiction typically involves a young adult transitioning into adulthood, Subhi's character arc contains many elements of a coming-of-age plot, and it could be said that having a pre-teen protagonist undergo this transformation highlights how detention forces children to grow up too quickly, robs them of innocence and interrupts healthy development.

Structure

Point of view

Point of view is pivotal to the structure of *The Bone Sparrow* as it links two parallel plot lines. The primary plot line is Subhi's, narrated in the first person. The secondary is Jimmie's, narrated in third-person limited voice. The use of alternating narrators draws thematic links between Subhi's and Jimmie's stories.

Dramatic arc

Nineteenth-century German writer Gustav Freytag developed a structural framework for narratives known as **Freytag's pyramid**, which has become a popular model for devising and analysing narratives. It identifies five parts of the **dramatic arc** or plot, which map the rise and fall of tension. This structure is evident in *The Bone Sparrow*.

Exposition: Subhi's and Jimmie's lives before they meet are described; both are battling grief and disadvantage. Jimmie's first visit to the centre is the inciting incident.

Rising action: Complications build through Jimmie and Subhi's budding friendship, Eli's transfer to Alpha, Subhi's escape to help a gravely ill Jimmie, and the frictions that lead to the protest.

Climax: A riot breaks out. Beaver kills Eli.

Falling action: The riot ends, guards cover up Eli's murder and investigators arrive as Subhi grapples with whether or not to speak up.

Denouement (resolution): Subhi tells the truth and prepares to testify. He reconnects with his family and finds renewed hope in telling Eli's story.

Temporal structure

The novel is written in the present tense. While the plot is linear, events from Subhi's and Jimmie's pasts are provided through flashbacks. Rather than constructing scenes from different points in time, Fraillon utilises present moments as triggers for memories that fill in background details and develop themes.

Story within a story

Parallel to the main narrative is the story of Anka and Oto. Presented as entries in Jimmie's mother's notebook, the story symbolises Jimmie's connection to her mother. This device draws parallels between Subhi's and Jimmie's histories, while the fact that Jimmie's ancestors originate from outside Australia reminds readers that, aside from Australia's First Nations peoples, all Australians have come from elsewhere. This celebrates Australia's multicultural diversity and challenges the perceptions of a homogenous Australian population that often underpin anti-refugee attitudes.

Circularity

Circularity involves stories ending where they began, and *The Bone Sparrow* utilises symbolic circularity. Both the first and final chapters reference the Night Sea and Maá's ability to see and hear the things Subhi imagines; each asks the other if they can 'hear it, *né*?' (p.1, p.228). Maá's ability to perceive Subhi's imagined world in the final chapter contrasts with her mental state at other points in the story, conveying her renewed hope. Both chapters also refer to Eli's whale. In the beginning, this represents Eli's affection for Subhi. In the final chapter the symbolism has evolved and we understand that Eli's story will live on through Subhi.

Style and language

Subhi's voice

Subhi's voice expresses his perspective and personality. He is an **unreliable narrator** because of his naivety, and readers can infer things he does not understand. His dreamy, optimistic tone emphasises his innocence and resilience.

Subhi's childlike voice is constructed through **idiolect** (the unique speech pattern of an individual). He uses simple, direct language, such as 'Eli reckons' (p.65) and 'doesn't matter one bit' (p.152), and describes his emotions in terms of physical sensations, such as 'fizzing' (p.182) and 'burning' (p.140). Subhi also frequently uses adjectives as nouns that emphasise his sensory and emotional experiences. Examples include: 'there's a sick going around' (p.123) and 'full of happy' (p.125). A **synecdoche** is a figure of speech in which a part of something is used to represent the whole, such as Subhi referring to guards as 'Jackets' and the world beyond the fences as 'the Outside'. 'Someday' is a powerful example as it refers to the future with low modality (lack of certainty). It shows that Subhi maintains hope for freedom, even though there is no certainty about when, or if, that will happen. Just as these are capitalised, so are many other common nouns, such as features of the setting (Rec Room, Hard Road), and items or concepts such as Pebbles of Happy, the Night Sea, the Bone Sparrow and Towers of Rah. This elevates each subject, reminding us how insular Subhi's world is and how seemingly trivial things have a substantial impact on him.

Humour

The Shakespeare duck often delivers comical wisecracks, and many characters tell jokes. Humour works to lighten the tone and counterbalance the more confronting elements of the novel, which is important given the target audience. It also reminds us of the power of humour to help people cope with stress and to foster social connections.

Symbolism

Fraillon uses several symbols in addition to the Bone Sparrow, the Night Sea and Eli's whale. Subhi refers to the children in detention as 'Limbo kids' (p.11), alluding to the Catholic concept of 'Limbo' (a region between heaven and hell) and carrying the connotation of people being 'cast out' into an endless oblivion. Subhi, Eli and Jimmie have objects they treasure that symbolise their love for deceased family members. **Birds** symbolise life, freedom and journeys. The **earth** represents the fact that, beyond the borders that divide people, we live on the same earth, as a single human race.

Some symbols carry multiple meanings. The symbolism of the Night Sea taps into the **duality** of water. Subhi's family fled Myanmar by boat across dangerous oceans, and yet the Night Sea is a cleansing force that empowers Subhi. This duality is also evident in the rains that both terrify and refresh. Likewise, **rats** are predominantly considered vermin and their presence exemplifies the unsanitary conditions; Queeny uses rats as a metaphor for anti-refugee attitudes. However, Subhi and Jimmie see rats as deserving of the same respect and care as any other creature. Lastly, **rocks** are able to be manipulated by people for good and evil purposes – as tools for play, to save Jimmie and to murder Eli. These dualities draw attention to the subjectivity of people's attitudes and choices, inviting readers to question beliefs and attitudes that appear normalised, and to contemplate the responsibility of individuals to consider how their choices can either contribute to or combat injustice.

Motifs

A **motif** is a repeated image, symbol or phrase, often used as a structural device to thread together elements of plot and develop themes. The title informs readers that the Bone Sparrow is central to the narrative and, as the plot progresses, repeated references to sparrows and Jimmie's necklace allow the motif to gather meaning. The necklace and its origin story are central to Jimmie and Subhi's relationship, and function as a symbol of hope, safety, freedom, family and unity.

The Night Sea initially symbolises Subhi's optimism. As tensions in the camp rise and Subhi's hopefulness is challenged, the Night Sea loses some of its power to soothe but finally returns, bringing Eli's whale and helping Subhi find the courage to speak up.

Imagery

Descriptive details of mould, fences, security cameras, contaminated food, filthy toilets and cramped tents evoke the horrific conditions of the camp. The contrast with descriptions of Jimmie's world on the other side of the fences – the lemon tree, Jimmie swimming in a river and climbing a gum tree, her soft bed – emphasise the disparity between Jimmie's and Subhi's circumstances.

CHAPTER-BY-CHAPTER ANALYSIS

Chapter One (pp.1–8)

Summary: *Subhi wakes one morning to find a shell that he believes was washed up by an imaginary Night Sea.*

Juxtaposition between the Night Sea and the setting immediately conveys the inhumanity of detention. Subhi's family is fractured by Maá's depression and Queeny's cynicism. Subhi's Night Sea provides an escape from the horrors of his life and, with his unwavering belief that his father will rejoin the family one day, readers understand Subhi has hope for a better future.

Key point

Subhi refers to Maá's condition as 'tired days' (p.2), implying he is too young to understand what is happening to her. However, the details given signify to readers that she is likely suffering severe depression. This is an all-too-common reality for refugees who have escaped traumatic situations only to find themselves detained for long periods without access to adequate health services.

Key vocabulary

Ba: a Rohingya term for father.

Maá: a Rohingya term for mother.

Né: an interrogative term in Rohingya, used at the end of a question.

Q Which details reflect the horrific conditions of detention centres in Australia?

Q How does Subhi's voice convey hope and resilience?

Chapter Two (pp.9–18)

Summary: *Harvey brings a paddling pool; Subhi meets the Shakespeare duck and finds a sparrow on his bed.*

The opening line is darker than that of Chapter One, and the oppressive heat emphasises suffering. The pool conveys Harvey's benevolence and his presence makes 'the grumping itch' in Subhi's head disappear, establishing that the guard's friendship comforts Subhi (p.11).

Subhi's and Queeny's contrasting attitudes to the duck reflect their different outlooks, which are reinforced in this chapter. Subhi's innocence and desire for freedom are conveyed by descriptions of him playing and holding his head under water. Queeny's belief that the sparrow is an omen of death is another example of her fearful outlook and concludes the chapter on a dark note.

Q How is setting constructed through the line 'it's only breakfast time, but already the sun looks angry' (p.10)?

Q Why do you think Fraillon included the detail about the magazines in the Rec Room?

Chapter Three (pp.19–22)

Summary: *Jimmie is introduced to readers on the third anniversary of her mother's death.*

Immediately it is clear Jimmie has much in common with Subhi – both have experienced loss and have a grief-stricken parent. Jimmie's inability to read is a source of pain because she cannot read her mother's notebook and 'hear her mum's voice again' (p.22). The novel's title is referenced in Jimmie's necklace, indicating that it will play an important role in the narrative.

Q How does the Bone Sparrow necklace compare and contrast with the sparrow in Chapter Two? How does this draw parallels between Subhi and Jimmie?

Chapter Four (pp.23–30)

Summary: *Subhi helps Eli run packages around the camp but is thwarted by Beaver.*

Subhi's concerns about the sparrow are forgotten when he goes on a package run for Eli. We get a sense of Eli's savviness and genuine affection for Subhi, while Subhi's matter-of-fact descriptions of the setting suggest the prison-like environment is 'normal' to him, despite being incongruous with readers' notions of a safe place for children. The mood shifts when Subhi notices 'the way the scared covers Pietre's face' (p.29) and he realises his carelessness has put him in danger. Subhi's terror at the sight of Beaver establishes the guard as the antagonist.

Key point

Deprivation is emphasised with the revelation that detainees trade items just to acquire basic necessities. The indifferent and callous attitude of some guards is indicated when they deny detainees their allotted two bottles of drinking water and tip their water out if they complain.

Q How does Eli's attitude to the sparrow differ from Subhi's and Queeny's, and what does this suggest about him?

Q What impression do you get of Beaver from the phrase 'sour smoke smell' (p.30)?

Chapter Five (pp.31–8)

Summary: *Queeny saves Subhi from Beaver; Subhi recalls his mother's stories.*

Subhi's nightmares and the image of Beaver slamming Subhi into the wall confirm Beaver's role as antagonist. We see Queeny's protectiveness when she lies to Beaver and puts Subhi to bed. Subhi recalls Maá's 'Listen Now stories' (p.36) and, even though she no longer shares them, Subhi requests one every night, fearing she might lose herself if she forgets them. Subhi wakes in the night to the realisation that he had fallen asleep without asking her.

Q What does Subhi mean when he says, at the end of the chapter, 'and then everything changed' (p.38)?

Chapter Six (pp.39–45)

Summary: *Jimmie is confused by rumours about the detention centre and decides to find out the truth.*

Much of this chapter is retrospective, providing exposition of Jimmie's background. The imagery of the garden is lush and colourful, suggesting that, for Jimmie, losing her mother meant losing comfort and joy. Descriptions of the town reveal economic strain and isolation. When Jimmie's classmates complain about detainees getting free things, readers are shown how misinformation can impact community attitudes. Jimmie's recollection of her mother's compassion for the detainees causes her to doubt the veracity of these rumours.

Q Why does Jimmie think 'reading is important' but school is not (p.39)?

Q What does it mean that Jimmie's father 'never seemed to really notice much these days' (p.40)?

Chapter Seven (pp.46–51)

Summary: *Subhi wishes for the Night Sea to wash away his fear; while the others sleep, he creeps out of the tent and meets Jimmie.*

When the Night Sea does not come to wash away his worries as he wishes, Subhi leaves the tent and finds Jimmie. He feels an instant affinity with her when she pushes her hand into the dirt, making him wonder if she 'listens to the earth' like Maá says he does (p.49). He thinks she might be a guardian angel, emphasising the magical quality of her sudden appearance. Jimmie asks if they have bikes in the centre but

Subhi's only knowledge of bikes is from stories, revealing more about his deprivation. Jimmie and Subhi each have something special to offer the other – Jimmie's mother's stories and Subhi's ability to read – which is a catalyst to bring them together again.

Q What is the symbolic meaning of Subhi thinking Jimmie's appearance is 'like that red dirt had up and whooshed her straight from the ground' (p.48)?

Chapter Eight (pp.52–61)

Summary: *Eli is enraged about Beaver, gives Subhi stolen muesli bars and learns he is being moved to Alpha Compound.*

Eli's rage contrasts with his previously jovial nature, conveying his protectiveness of Subhi. The guard's arrival prompts Subhi to think Eli is going to be released, making the revelation of Eli's illogical transfer more disheartening. The reference to a boy who previously faced a similar situation and experienced such trauma that he tried to take his own life is a shocking detail that paints a harrowing picture of the impact of detention on children.

Key point

Metonymy is a figurative device that involves referring to a subject through a closely related thing; for example, 'the crown' meaning the king or queen. In this chapter, the 'writing' that 'lies all the time' (p.58) is a metonym for the bureaucratic policies and procedures that impact detainees.

Q What traits, values and attitudes are displayed when Queeny stands up to the guard?

Q How do Eli, Subhi and Queeny's fantasies highlight the cruelty of detention?

Chapter Nine (pp.62–4)

Summary: *Jimmie reflects on meeting Subhi.*

While short, this chapter presents a pivotal moment in the plot when Jimmie decides to return to the centre so Subhi can read her mother's book to her.

Q What new details do we learn about Jimmie and her life?

Chapter Ten (pp.65–77)

Summary: *Subhi struggles to adjust to life without Eli; Jimmie visits again.*

The loss of Eli's protection makes Subhi the target of teens who steal his clothes and shoes, and demand he hand over the package business supplies. While Subhi admits most things to Eli, he withholds being forced to kill a baby rat, revealing his shame about not standing up to the older children.

Jimmie's return thrills Subhi. She offers friendship and excitement at a difficult time in his life. She presents her mother's notebook, forging the bond between them. Seeing the Bone Sparrow fills Subhi with fear and their contrasting interpretations of its symbolism emphasise their vastly different outlooks and life experiences.

Q How do Subhi's and Harvey's contrasting views about rats emphasise Subhi's perspective?

Q Why does Eli lie about wanting to give up the package business?

Q In what ways are Subhi and Jimmie similar?

Chapter Eleven (pp.78–81)

Summary: *Subhi reads from Jimmie's mother's notebook for the first time.*

The first entry in the notebook is about Anka, a baby 'born from an egg' (p.78), who is immediately loved by six-year-old Oto. Subhi is frustrated when the entry ends abruptly but Jimmie wishes to save the rest for another time, wanting to prolong the experience of finally hearing her mother's words. She leaves, giving Subhi the feather she's been holding, a symbol connecting Jimmie to the bird-like Anka and a memento of the pivotal moment Subhi and Jimmie have shared.

Q What bird-related imagery appears in this chapter and how does this develop ideas already introduced?

Q What does it mean that Anka is 'destined to see more than most' (p.80)?

Chapter Twelve (pp.82–3)

Summary: *Jimmie returns home and sleeps well for the first time since losing her mother.*

When her brother Jonah suggested their mother's stories were childish, Jimmie wanted to appear grown up and echoed his sentiments. But her mother continued to whisper the stories to Jimmie at night, knowing that deep down Jimmie still believed. Even though she knows the stories by heart, Jimmie is delighted to have heard her mother's voice come alive through Subhi.

Q At the end of the chapter, 'Jimmie sleeps the long, deep sleep of someone who has finally found what they are looking for' (p.83). What has Jimmie found and why might that allow her to sleep well?

Chapter Thirteen (pp.84–91)

Summary: *On his birthday, Subhi eats well, receives gifts, spends time with Nasir and enjoys a special moment with Maá.*

With guests visiting the centre, meals improve and, despite the ulterior motives behind this, the detainees relish the pleasure of nourishing food. We learn more about the inhumane conditions of the centre, such as detainees being denied medical equipment and medicine.

Subhi's gratitude for the modest gifts he receives shows his humility. Themes of hope and change are developed when Maá has a rare moment of lucidity and tells Subhi a new story about rain breaking a drought when he was born.

Q Why are Nasir's stones called 'Pebbles of Happy' and why are they so important to Subhi?

Q What symbolic meaning is conveyed through Subhi's birth story?

Chapter Fourteen (pp.92–102)

Summary: *Jimmie brings hot chocolate and Subhi reads a second Bone Sparrow story.*

Jimmie bringing hot chocolate is a small act of kindness that has a big impact. Jimmie describes her bedroom; this is the first time Subhi learns anything about the world outside the fences. She promises to someday show him everything, indicating her desire for a long friendship with him. They give each other pen tattoos and Subhi tells Jimmie Eli's whale story; we see how their friendship provides each with normal childhood experiences they were previously denied. Subhi reads of Oto and Anka marrying and their 'charmed life' being disrupted by war (p.99). This allegorises the refugee issue, reminding readers that war and conflict impact innocent people.

Q Why do the guards laugh when Queeny gets angry with them? What does it mean that 'they don't laugh with their eyes' (p.93)?

Q Why does Jimmie give Subhi the torch?

Chapter Fifteen (pp.103–4)

Summary: *Jimmie returns home and concocts a plan to show Subhi the world outside the fences.*

At the beginning of the chapter, Jimmie 'lets loose a long howl of happiness', indicating a significant change in her mood. Her elation disappears when she considers the 'unfairness' of Subhi's life, revealing her compassion and empathy (p.103). She takes Jonah's old phone so she can show Subhi her life. Feeling a new sense of belonging, Jimmie does not sleep with her mum's book. Instead, she puts it in her drawer, 'waiting for Subhi to share it with' (p.104). This suggests her friendship with Subhi has begun to heal her broken heart.

Q Jimmie wants to show Subhi 'everything he's going to see' (p.104). How does her hopeful attitude suggest a degree of naivety? How does this influence your response to Subhi's situation?

Chapter Sixteen (pp.105–11)

Summary: *Queeny acquires a camera and Subhi has a startling realisation about the future.*

Subhi is frustrated as Eli plots with Queeny; Subhi's inability to understand his sister reflects his naivety and innocence. While Queeny is only a little older, she understands their injustice more deeply and is desperate to fight back. When Subhi thinks that Eli is 'beginning to sound a lot like Queeny', it becomes clear Eli's cheeriness is eroding (p.106). Subhi reflects on the past when Queeny taught other children to read and played games. The changes in Eli and Queeny emphasise how detention robs children of innocence. Subhi laments Queeny no longer thinking of 'Someday', but comes to realise she is in fact focused on the future, just not in the same way that he is. This realisation is a pivotal moment in his coming-of-age arc.

Key point

This chapter uses retrospection to reference contextual issues such as media restrictions, the banning of cameras and breaches of children's rights. While Subhi does not always comprehend the complexities of the system, he knows that he and his family 'aren't wanted in this place, or in Burma, or in any other place' (p.110).

Q How does the narrative point of view in this chapter imply Subhi's childlike view of complex issues? What does the reader understand that Subhi does not?

Chapter Seventeen (pp.112–22)

Summary: *Nasir dies; Jimmie visits and Subhi touches the soil on the Outside.*

Subhi is devastated by Nasir's death and insulted by the immediate reallocation of his bed. Jimmie's photos of the Outside open up a whole new world to Subhi. They read about Anka being captured by soldiers and Oto commencing a journey to find her. Jimmie's influence on Subhi is suggested through his changing perception of the Bone Sparrow. Jimmie shows Subhi where she enters the facility and invites him to leave with her. He refuses but his hand touches the soil on the other side of the fence, making his first ever contact with the world outside.

Q How are descriptive details used to juxtapose Subhi's and Jimmie's living situations?

Q How does Subhi's comment that 'there isn't much soft in here' convey both the literal and symbolic meanings of detention (p.115)?

Q Why do you think Subhi chooses not to leave?

Chapter Eighteen (pp.123–34)

Summary: *The detainees have food poisoning; Jimmie visits and tells Subhi his future; they read of Oto's journey.*

The food-poisoning incident corresponds with a rise in tension in the air, indicating this event is a significant trigger for the upcoming protest. Queeny tells Subhi she's 'sick of being invisible' (p.125) and we see a change in Subhi when he realises what she means. Jimmie's friendship has shown him what it means to be seen and heard, which feels good, but also 'makes it worse' by opening his eyes to the reality of marginalisation (p.126). Consequently, not wanting to know his future when playing the 'P.R.I.V.A.T.E.' game suggests a loss of idealism (p.129).

Anka gives birth and Oto hears her 'love song' from across the country. He continues his journey wearing the Bone Sparrow for 'luck and protection' (p.131). Meeting Iliya bolsters his hope of finding his family, but when Iliya steps on a mine both he and the Bone Sparrow's green coin disappear, and Oto must continue alone. The story triggers Subhi's anxiety about Ba, but Jimmie's presence gives him comfort.

Q What do you think is the cause of the 'sad angry that's floating all over' (p.125)?

Q What does the simile 'happiness whispered up into the air like water on a hot day' suggest about what happens to new arrivals (pp.125–6)?

Key vocabulary

P.R.I.V.A.T.E. game: a children's game that predicts the player's future; when Subhi plays, the game predicts his future profession will be storyteller.

Chapter Nineteen (pp.135–44)

Summary: *Maá is put on HRAT Watch; Eli learns he may be sent to an offshore facility; the protest begins.*

This chapter further humanises refugees by showing the impact of people smuggling, ocean journeys and offshore processing. Subhi misses Maá and the focus on her voice draws parallels between her and Anka. Subhi recalls a line from one of Maá's songs: '*If we all sing together, our song can light up the dark*' (p.138). This is repeated in Chapter Thirty-Three and reinforces the values of unity and harmony.

A sparrow inspires Subhi to show Eli where he can escape. Eli's response that he 'can't bugger off and leave everyone' conveys his loyalty to his fellow detainees (p.140). The protest begins and Queeny takes a photo to send to the media. While the protestors appear united and determined, Subhi has a sense of foreboding.

Key vocabulary

HRAT Watch: supervision by the High Risk and Trauma team.

Key point

Sewing one's lips together is a common protest strategy used by refugees in detention around the world. It is an extreme form of hunger strike and reflects their feeling of having been silenced.

Q What is the symbolic significance of Subhi imagining 'Eli's whale thrashing about and bellowing long howls into the wind' (p.143)?

Q The chapter ends with everyone awake and waiting to 'listen to the earth again' (p.144). What does this suggest?

Chapter Twenty (pp.145–7)

Summary: *Jimmie sees a photo of the detainees' hunger strike in the newspaper.*

Jimmie's teacher gives her a book and asks if anyone is at 'home to help her read it', suggesting she knows a little of Jimmie's situation (p.145). Jimmie sees Queeny's photo of protesters in the newspaper and feels the same sense that 'something bad is coming' that Subhi had, reinforcing the foreboding mood (p.146). Jimmie's father's empathy for the detainees contrasts with the envious attitudes of Jimmie's peers at school (p.43). Jimmie struggles to understand why the refugees are detained.

Q Do you think offering prizes addresses the causes of poor school attendance in regional areas?

Q The questions Jimmie wants to ask about the refugees (pp.146–7) are pivotal to the themes of the novel. Read them and consider the different answers you might receive from Jimmie's parents, Subhi, Queeny, Harvey and Beaver, or even from a government representative or refugee advocate.

Chapter Twenty-One (pp.148–53)

Summary: *Jimmie brings Subhi a feast and he helps her read her schoolbook.*

Despondent after seeing Queeny's photograph in the paper, Jimmie brings Subhi a feast in an attempt to bring him joy. Subhi's tears reveal conflicting emotions – guilt, shame, happiness and gratitude – indicating another moment of discovery in which his exhilaration is marred by harsh realities.

Jimmie recounts her mother singing to her plants, drawing links to Anka and Maá, and conveying ideas about family, mothers and the power of song. Subhi helps Jimmie read her schoolbook, their friendship deepening as they find new ways to care for each other. Subhi puts a napkin in his pocket so he can keep a piece of the feast and Jimmie with him. Forgetting to read Jimmie's mother's book is another indication of the deepening bond between the pair, which now extends beyond the exchange of reading and stories.

Q Jimmie says 'I hear you' to Subhi (p.149), which echoes her father's dialogue in Chapter Twenty. What is the correlation between 'being heard' and the experiences of detainees?

Chapter Twenty-Two (pp.154–6)

Summary: *Jimmie visits the attic, finds her mother's garden gnome, Old Gnome, and cuts her arm on a shard of metal.*

Entering the attic is a pivotal moment in Jimmie's healing. Her interactions with Old Gnome mirror Subhi's with the Shakespeare duck, signifying that Jimmie is rediscovering a sense of wonder because of Subhi. Singing, which represents Jimmie's connection with her mother, is referenced again. Licking the cut on her arm alludes to previous comments about germs and cleaning wounds, indicating Jimmie's naivety and foreshadowing danger.

Q What details in this chapter imply that Jimmie's relationship with Subhi is helping her to heal?

Chapter Twenty-Three (pp.157–63)

Summary: *Queeny blames Subhi for the camera being confiscated by Harvey and destroys Subhi's drawings in retaliation; Subhi finds a knife in the sand.*

Subhi's lasting memories and feeling of fullness emphasise the impact of Jimmie's kindness and he draws a picture to repay her, conveying humility and gratitude. His reference to drawing for the older detainees and the blanket metaphor develop the themes of the novel, emphasising the importance of listening to other people's stories.

Queeny's assumption that Subhi told Harvey about the camera reminds us she is just a child, despite frequently acting much older. Destroying Subhi's pictures is an attack on his imagination, innocence and optimism – qualities stolen from her by life in detention. This progression of conflict between Queeny and Subhi represents the deepening fractures in their family unit due to living in detention.

Subhi laments how much has changed recently and reveals that more detainees are joining the protest. Finding the knife escalates tension, foreshadowing danger.

Q Where else in the novel does Fraillon refer to 'whumping' (p.160) and what does this mean?

Q How does the style of Subhi's narration on pages 162–3 convey his naivety and suggest that moving the knife might not be a good idea?

Chapter Twenty-Four (pp.164–6)

Summary: *Jimmie is sick and her father leaves to work his final shift.*

The doona cover from Jimmie's father is another use of the bird motif and conveys that he understands her need to connect to her mother's stories.

His new job is a turning point, indicating that their family will soon be reunited. However, his needing to do one more shift away unsettles Jimmie and, given her sickness, suggests things might get worse before they getter better.

Q What clues are provided in previous chapters to suggest that Jimmie's illness is not the flu, and how does this create suspense? How do these clues add to your understanding of Jimmie's family's situation and the issues they face?

Chapter Twenty-Five (pp.167–73)

Summary: *Subhi hides the knife; Jimmie's infection worsens.*

A nervous energy envelops the centre as the protest continues to grow, indicating that hostilities are escalating. Subhi hides the knife but his anxiety persists. His thinking that Eli would know what to do is ironic once later events are revealed and reminds us of Subhi's childlike understanding of situations. Sniffing the napkin triggers memories of Jimmie's feast and is a way for Subhi to cope with the turbulence around him. It also creates a moment of calm, heightened through the banter with the duck. This moment of calmness contrasts with Jimmie's arrival, enhancing the effect of rising tension when we realise she is seriously ill.

Q What is the significance of Subhi calling the knife a 'treasure' (p.168)?

Q How does the imagery of the space behind the toilet add to your understanding of Subhi and his life?

Chapter Twenty-Six (pp.174–5)

Summary: *Jimmie is locked out of her house.*

Jimmie returns home, her condition deteriorating, and finds herself locked out. Details about her town and her father's job that were established earlier add to the tension as her isolation and her father's absence put

Jimmie in danger. Her only hope is to get Subhi's attention, but the reality that he is in a high-security facility and may not even be near the fence to see the torch flashing suggests hope is slim.

Q How does diction, sentence length and punctuation in this chapter help to convey Jimmie's emotions and deteriorating health?

Chapter Twenty-Seven (pp.176–9)

Summary: *Subhi reads the final Bone Sparrow story and sees Jimmie's torch flashing.*

Subhi finds the final Bone Sparrow story, which mirrors his own desires – to cheat fate, be free from captivity and reunite with Ba. The power of Anka's song contrasts with Maá's loss of song, making another correlation between songs and motherly love. Subhi finding the final story under a recipe implies that new chapters in life are always possible and that sometimes hope is found where it is least expected.

Subhi yearns to share the story with Jimmie, understanding that she, too, needs to know fate can be cheated. He sees her torch signal and instantly realises she needs help, but hesitates and misses his chance to escape.

Q What does Oto say to his son when he gives him the necklace? How does this develop themes from other parts of the novel?

Chapter Twenty-Eight (pp.180–6)

Summary: *The protestors barricade themselves inside Alpha; Subhi escapes to help Jimmie.*

The searchlights have been on all night, preventing Subhi from reaching Jimmie. Queeny's apology paves the way for reconciling with Subhi but her mood turns when the Jackets retrieve their riot gear. The image of traumatised children screaming emphasises how detention exacerbates their distress. Subhi perceives Queeny's anger as a return to bossiness, but it is clear she is frightened and trying to protect him. When he accuses her of not caring she is deeply hurt, described by way of a simile that references Beaver slapping a mother. This brings Beaver to mind, reminding us of his cruelty and adding tension by inviting us to consider how he might behave in a riot. While the commotion distracts everyone, Subhi escapes the centre for the very first time.

Q How do the chapter's opening sentences convey regret, and how does this sense of regret relate to other moments in Subhi's narrative?

Q There are many phrases in this chapter that have been used elsewhere. What are they and what is the effect of their repetition?

Chapter Twenty-Nine (pp.187–93)

Summary: *Subhi finds Jimmie and calls for help; on returning to the centre, he climbs a tree and sees a fire has broken out.*

Subhi finds Jimmie and breaks into her house with a rock. He remembers how to apply first aid from reading the Emergency Folder. There is an irony in this – depriving children of books and education limits their power, but Subhi's persistence means he learned something that could save a life. Subhi reads the final Bone Sparrow story to Jimmie, hoping that knowing its ending will bring her luck. He hides when the ambulance arrives and watches as Jonah returns with chocolate and a bicycle. By following through on his promise, Jonah conveys his love for Jimmie despite the fact that he wasn't there when she was in danger. Climbing a tree, Subhi looks around him and notices the fire at the centre. The momentary freedom Subhi experiences being in the Outside and at the top of the tree is juxtaposed with the chaos erupting in the centre.

Q What scares Subhi when he is in the tree?

Q Why do you think he does not 'feel' free when he is physically out of confinement (p.192)?

Chapter Thirty (pp.194–9)

Summary: *A riot has broken out and the centre is burning; Beaver murders Eli as Harvey and Subhi watch on.*

The centre is in chaos and the fences have come down, symbolising the protestors' uprising against the forces that imprison them. Subhi's willingness to sizzle up 'like a sausage' (p.194) with Maá and Queeny emphasises his loyalty to and need for his family. Subhi watches as Eli is unable to defend himself from Beaver because Subhi has moved his knife. This refers back to Chapter Twenty-Five, activating the irony of the twist that the knife belongs to Eli and enhancing the tragedy of the scene. Beaver uses a rock to kill Eli, a juxtaposition with previous uses of rocks, such as when Subhi uses them to play games and to save Jimmie. Harvey's choice to follow Beaver at the end is a pivotal decision. Throughout the scene, Subhi is paralysed with regret for his passivity, echoing the incident with the baby rat.

Q When does Subhi realise moving the knife has put Eli in danger?

Q What is the significance of Beaver 'rubbing at that spot where his eye used to be' (p.199)?

Chapter Thirty-One (pp.200–1)

Summary: *Subhi recalls Eli escaping from his old country and witnessing his brother's death.*

Eli's escape story is a reminder of the dangerous journeys people are forced to take to seek safety from persecution and displacement. The chapter ends with Subhi reflecting on having 'thought' Eli's survival 'meant he had something important to do' (p.201). The word 'thought' indicates Subhi's sense of the injustice of Eli's death – he cheated fate only to have his life ended by Beaver before finishing his journey to freedom.

Q What is the effect of telling Eli's story at this point in the narrative?

Q Do you think Eli has achieved something important in his life?

Chapter Thirty-Two (pp.202–5)

Summary: *After the riot, Subhi struggles to accept that Harvey did not return with help and that Eli is dead.*

Subhi waits for Eli to move and Harvey to return, devastated when neither happens. Harvey interrogates him, his panic suggesting he is worried about Subhi's trauma after Eli's murder. However, he is likely also panicking about the possibility that Subhi saw Harvey there. This indicates a degree of guilt and shame. Subhi has the life-changing realisation that the world is much darker and more terrifying than he had ever imagined, and the phrase 'even my stories are gone' (p.205) implies he has lost all hope.

Q If Harvey is not angry with Subhi, who do you think he is angry with?

Chapter Thirty-Three (pp.206–13)

Summary: *Maá wakes; the guards concoct a cover-up story for Eli's death; Eli's whale helps Subhi make a difficult decision.*

Falling in and out of sleep, Subhi imagines Maá singing, recalling a time when her *taranas* united everyone and repeating the line from Chapter Nineteen: '*If we all sing together, our song can light up the dark*' (p.207). Subhi realises Maá is awake and singing for real, marking her return to him. Subhi is heartbroken on discovering Harvey's silent support of the Jackets' conspiracy to blame Eli for the riot and protect Beaver. Harvey again tries to ascertain what Subhi saw, discovers Subhi was there and tearfully professes that he tried to help. Subhi realises he has a difficult choice to make – protect Harvey and let Beaver get away with Eli's murder, or speak up and betray Harvey. When the Night Sea comes, Eli's whale appears and helps Subhi realise he must tell the truth.

Q Where else in the novel does Subhi express regret for inaction?

Q How does this chapter reveal a change in Subhi? What role does the Shakespeare duck play?

Chapter Thirty-Four (pp.214–17)

Summary: *Subhi learns Ba is dead and the Night Sea treasures were left by Queeny; Queeny gives Subhi the final treasure – Ba's book of poetry.*

Queeny and Subhi reconcile when Queeny admits she should have listened to Subhi about Jimmie. When she tells Subhi she was behind Ba's treasures, Subhi thinks it 'makes them even more special' (p.214), suggesting he finally realises how much she loves him. Receiving Ba's book helps Subhi feel closer to his father. The revelation that dead fish have appeared in the camp conveys the idea that unexpected things can happen, suggesting Subhi's life can improve. The fish remind Queeny of the Night Sea, indicating that she is gaining some of Subhi's optimism.

Q What does Ba's poem say about Subhi's connection to his father?

Q How do the language and imagery in the poem emphasise important ideas?

Chapter Thirty-Five (pp.218–21)

Summary: *Jimmie returns and Subhi writes the story of how Eli died.*

We learn that Jimmie has survived and that her father has returned home. Her transformation is complete now that she no longer needs the 'luck and protection' of the Bone Sparrow (p.219). Her calling Subhi a 'superhero' mirrors Subhi's thought that Jimmie is a 'guardian angel after all', signifying that they have saved each other (p.220). Jimmie gives Subhi a new way of thinking about the sparrow that appeared in Chapter Two, suggesting that it means change and rebirth and thus is a symbol of hope. As a result, Subhi finds the courage to write down Eli's story.

Q What do you think it means that Jimmie left the Thermos behind and that this thaws Subhi out 'from the inside' (p.220)?

Chapter Thirty-Six (pp.222–4)

Summary: *Subhi makes a report to investigators, sees Harvey for the last time and imagines the rest of Iliya's story.*

As Subhi goes to give his statement to investigators, Harvey nods his understanding, indicating his willingness to accept the consequences for his part in Eli's murder and the cover-up. Subhi imagines the end of Iliya's story, drawing links between his family and Jimmie's and reinforcing ideas about unity, freedom and family. The phrases 'a truly charmed life' and 'journey to peace' (p.224) refer back to Chapter Fourteen and Chapter Thirty-Three respectively.

Q Why does Subhi say he misses Harvey while looking at him?

Q How does Subhi's version of Iliya's story reflect Subhi's values and desires? Find the references to earlier chapters echoed here and consider how this repetition enhances specific ideas.

Chapter Thirty-Seven (pp.225–8)

Summary: *Subhi, Maá and Queeny watch lights dancing in the sky.*

Subhi, Maá and Queeny climb onto a container to watch the sky, indicating their reunification. Eli had once said it was impossible to see the sea from the centre, so when they each see the sea in the lights, Maá says it is proof that 'not ever can always change'. She holds a letter that has made her smile 'her biggest smile' (p.226), signifying renewed hope and hinting that positive change is coming. Subhi is ready to testify about Eli's death and finally feels brave like Ba. His transformation is complete now his family is hopeful again and he has found the courage to take action. The chapter ends with a reference to Eli's whale, symbolising Eli living on in his stories – the whale story Subhi will always hold onto and the story of his death that Subhi will share with the world.

Q What might Maá's letter say and why does Fraillon omit details?

Q How does the ending suggest that Eli did have something important to do, as Subhi had believed (p.201)?

CHARACTERS & RELATIONSHIPS

Subhi

Key quotes

'Sometimes, at night, the dirt outside turns into a beautiful ocean.' (p.1)

'Every time they tell a story, those words make those joinings-up bigger and louder and stronger, so that soon everyone will see and hear the way the whole world is joined up together by millions of tiny scraps.' (p.158)

'… I have to write the most important story of them all. The story which isn't even a story. The story that has to be told, no matter how hard it is to tell.' (p.221)

Fraillon utilises well-known character types, also known as 'archetypes', throughout her novel. As the protagonist, Subhi echoes the 'Everyman Hero' archetype. He is a relatable character who lacks the extraordinary abilities of a classical hero or superhero. As an underdog who has heroism thrust upon him, his moral compass and selflessness are key to his victory. Other examples of this archetype include Arthur Dent in *The Hitchhiker's Guide to the Galaxy* by Douglas Adams, Frodo Baggins in *The Lord of the Rings* by JRR Tolkien, and Marty McFly in the *Back to the Future* film trilogy, directed by Robert Zemeckis.

The opening sentence describes Subhi's Night Sea, evoking a whimsical mood and thoughts of freedom, peace and vitality. We quickly learn that the reality of Subhi's world is the antithesis of this image. This juxtaposition conveys Subhi's resilience and suggests his imagination provides an escape from the atrocious conditions of the centre. This resilience is further conveyed through his innate optimism and belief that 'Someday' he will be with his father and his family will be free.

Subhi is an ordinary child: he plays games, draws, and values his friends and family. However, as a 'Limbo kid' his future is uncertain. Born on Australian soil but not an Australian, and feeling disconnected from his Rohingya heritage, he exists on the periphery of two cultures with no land to call home. Despite his circumstances, he is empathetic and caring. He endeavours to look after Maá, draws pictures for the older detainees and hopes that one day the whole world will hear the stories of those in need and be united. These positive qualities endear Subhi to readers, so that, as we see his optimism and hope wane, the injustice of detention is emphasised.

A series of life-altering events, including saving Jimmie's life, briefly tasting freedom only to have to return to captivity, watching Eli die, learning of Ba's death and incriminating Harvey, strip Subhi of his innocence and expose him to the harsh realities of the world. As a dynamic character (a character who demonstrates internal change), his developmental arc is central to the themes of the novel. He overcomes fear, shame and feelings of powerlessness when he finds the courage to take action by telling Eli's story.

Jimmie

Key quotes

'Jimmie wants to ask more. Wants to find out how they can help, so that no one has to sew their lips together. Wants to know why they have been locked up in there for so long. Why no one is listening. Why it is illegal for people to try to save their families. Why it is illegal to want to live.' (pp.146–7)

'Even though it seems kind of strange that a guardian angel would wear pants with more holes all over than mine even and a shirt that is way too big ...' (p.49)

Jimmie is described as a scruffy, spirited girl whose mother had nicknamed her 'Cyclone Jimmie' (p.63). Subhi's first observations are of her frizzy hair, dishevelled clothes and ability to hock up 'the biggest ball of snot' (p.49). These wild, untamed traits are reminiscent of 'The Innocent' archetype – a naive child who embodies sincerity, truthfulness and moral purity. This positions readers to trust Jimmie from the outset, priming us to accept the values and attitudes she embodies. Typical of 'The Innocent', Jimmie lives in a corrupt world but has not been sullied by its ills. She symbolises humanity in its purest form. Thus, when Jimmie questions her schoolmates' prejudices, and accepts Subhi with an open heart, the novel implies that discrimination and intolerance are learned attitudes that defy human nature.

Jimmie's family's hardships convey the theme of regional disadvantage; however, they also suggest that wealth and social status do not dictate a person's worth. Despite her having little in the way of wealth or social power, Jimmie's humble acts of kindness demonstrate the potency of empathy and compassion. Her attitudes offer a counterpoint to those underpinning Australia's detention policies, suggesting that the government, which has immense power and privilege, is ruthless and self-serving.

Jimmie's family

Key quotes

'Outside in the garden, she hears a howl, long and pained. Her dad is awake. Even through blocked ears Jimmie can hear him crying.' (p.22)

'When Jimmie hears the front door open and Jonah's voice singing along to the music blaring in his ears, she feels an excitement and a happiness buzz through her.' (p.62)

Jimmie's mother is portrayed as having been a warm, nurturing woman who made the family's home a place of safety and comfort. Since his wife's death, Jimmie's father has struggled with the burden of his grief and trying to fill the hole his wife left behind. Unable to leave the home his wife loved, Jimmie's father is forced to abandon the children to work shifts in another town, after losing his job when the local mines closed. At sixteen, Jonah is tasked with looking after his sister, but often falls short of this responsibility. Nonetheless, he is affectionate and loving, bringing her chocolate and following through on a promise to get her a new bike. Jimmie's loneliness eats away at her and the neglect she endures comes to a head when she almost dies of an infection. When her father finds work close to home, Jimmie feels safe and protected, and readers are given the sense that the family will finally be able to heal.

Jimmie and Subhi

Key quotes

'Jimmie hasn't sung a single note since her mum died, but when she opens her eyes, she realises it is her own voice she has been hearing.' (p.155)

'... I think of the different I feel when Jimmie is here. Like someone is really seeing me, really listening. I haven't felt like that before.' (p.126)

From the outset, Jimmie and Subhi each meet a need in the other: Jimmie offers Subhi access to the outside world, while Subhi's friendship alleviates Jimmie's loneliness and helps keep her mother's memory alive. The impact of their friendship is evident in each character's transformation. Jimmie finds happiness, allowing her to sleep well and sing for the first time since her mother's death. Subhi finds respite in Jimmie's company and experiences what it means to matter to someone from the Outside.

The Bone Sparrow story sparks their connection, but the parallels between Anka and Oto's story and Subhi's family remind us that family union and a safe home are fundamental human needs. The story has a mythical, timeless quality that depoliticises the novel's subject matter. This focuses readers' attention on the human element of events such as war and displacement by removing all the biases, fears and controversies surrounding refugees.

Jimmie and Subhi initially have conflicting beliefs about Jimmie's necklace and the meaning of sparrows. As Subhi reads Jimmie's story his view changes and he adopts her belief in the necklace as a symbol of luck and protection rather than a symbol of death. This change highlights the positive impact of Jimmie's friendship. Just as the Bone Sparrow was passed from Mirka to Oto, Oto to Iliya, Oto to his son and later from Jimmie's mother to Jimmie, Jimmie finally passes it to Subhi. With her father starting a job that allows him to finally return home for good, Jimmie no longer needs its powers. Giving Subhi a precious family heirloom is an act of love that ties them together, much like Subhi forming an ancestral link between their families when he imagines Iliya settling in Myanmar with the missing green coin that eventually washes up on the Night Sea as one of Ba's treasures.

Key point

The idea that the coin and sparrow are finally reunited represents the transformative power of Jimmie and Subhi's bond, implying humans need each other to survive and thrive. Underpinning this is the belief that we are one human race, inherently linked by history, nature, needs and desires. This promotes the values of unity, harmony and social cohesion, while condemning prejudice, segregation and intolerance.

Eli

Key quotes

'Eli stands up and smiles his big smile at the Jacket and when the Jacket turns around to go, Eli blows him a kiss.' (p.59)

'"I'm scared, Subhi. I don't want to go. I'm not a grown-up. I don't want to be one yet." Eli is crying. Eli who never shows his scared to anyone.' (p.139)

Eli's immediate family are deceased and for a period he lived with his uncle and cousins in detention, but has been alone since they left to reunite with 'their maá all the way on the other side of the world' (p.56). Eli keeps his brother's glove in his pocket as his only remaining connection to his family. Despite all his loss, he is spirited and cheeky, blowing kisses at the guards when their backs are turned and running the package business in defiance of the draconian regime operating at the centre. This business gives Eli a sense of purpose, both as a means of passing time and of supporting his fellow detainees by providing essential items such as toiletries and clothing.

At thirteen, he is on the cusp of adolescence. Playing games and joking around reveal his youthfulness, but he is markedly less naive and more self-sufficient than Subhi. He is cynical about Harvey and displays a keen savviness in keeping his business and supplies concealed from guards. He tends to shrug off worries and teaches Subhi to always hide his fear, but this changes after he is transferred to Alpha. Living with single men and away from families and children hardens him. His fearless mask cracks when he is faced with the possibility of being sent overseas, and he becomes increasingly sombre as he is drawn into the rising hostilities in the centre that result in his death.

Eli and Subhi

Key quotes

'Eli says we're more than best friends. We're brothers.' (p.4)

'It doesn't matter that Eli is lying through his teeth, as Harvey says, because Eli, he makes everything all right.' (p.68)

'I see every moment I ever had with Eli reflected in the whale's eyes and hear every word we ever spoke, every look, every laugh, echoing in the sound of the waves … and in the whale's eye I see exactly what I have to do. For Eli.' (pp.212–13)

Eli is more pragmatic than Subhi. He does not share Subhi's fanciful notions but never ridicules or belittles Subhi for his naivety. Telling the whale story shows Eli's desire to nurture and care for Subhi, even though he does not value stories the same way. He teaches Subhi games, how to tie shoelaces and ways to safely sneak around the camp. Fiercely protective, Eli is enraged when Beaver hurts Subhi and often tries to shield Subhi from the harsher realities of their lives. This becomes problematic when Subhi's ignorance leads him to move the knife that might have changed the outcome of Eli's confrontation with Beaver. The irony that Subhi's desire to keep others safe contributes to the death of his best friend emphasises that detention is no place for children.

The boys' bond is pivotal to Subhi's transformation. His love for Eli empowers him to overcome his fears as he realises that telling the truth is the only way to ensure Eli did not die in vain. The reversal of the relationship – from Subhi relying on Eli to Subhi being the one who seeks justice for Eli – encapsulates Subhi's coming of age as he finally finds a voice and a sense of autonomy.

Queeny and Subhi

Key quotes

'Queeny, she never tries to look in the shadows. She doesn't even squint.' (p.1)

'My treasures didn't come from the Night Sea at all. Or from my ba.
My treasures came from Queeny. Somehow that makes them even more special.' (p.214)

Even though her real name is Noor, everyone calls Subhi's sister Queeny. It is a fitting nickname given her austerity and disdain for all things childish. She is a foil to Subhi's character, emphasising his naivety and optimism through her cynicism, impatience and pessimism. Subhi mourns for the past when Queeny was affectionate and playful, and is frustrated by her short temper and bossiness. He sees these as flaws, unable to recognise her suffering or her attempts to protect him.

Their relationship exhibits many contradictions. Queeny calls Subhi 'stupid', tells him to grow up and punches him. However, she confronts Beaver to protect Subhi and secretly leaves out Ba's Night Sea treasures in an attempt to preserve Subhi's innocence and hope. Their conflicting views about the future emphasise their different attitudes. Subhi sees looking forward to 'Someday' as hopeful optimism, while Queeny sees taking action as necessary to make change.

By the end of the novel, they understand each other better. They resolve their conflicts when Queeny reveals the truth about Ba's death and Subhi's treasures. When Queeny reads Subhi the poem Ba wrote about him, it is implied that she has stopped taking her frustration out on Subhi and accepts him for who he is.

Maá and Subhi

Key quotes

'And then one day Maá stopped the stories. The good, happy ones as well. One day she just said, "No more. Looking back only brings sad, Subhi. Now look forward. No more back."' (p.36)

'Maá won't wake up. She's just stopped. Sometimes her eyes open, but she isn't really there. She isn't really seeing.' (p.135)

At the start of the novel, Maá displays symptoms of depression caused by the trauma of persecution and deportation, which have escalated after a decade in detention and the news of her husband's death. Her refusal to speak Rohingya or tell her stories signifies a loss of identity, and the irony that her decision to only look forward results in a devastating loss of all hope highlights the psychological battle refugees face in detention.

When Maá's health declines further, she is put on HRAT Watch, which devastates Subhi. Being deprived of his mother's comfort exacerbates his suffering, while his inability to help causes guilt and shame. After the riot, Harvey carries a traumatised Subhi to Maá, triggering her awakening. When she and Subhi hear Eli's whale singing in the final chapter, we sense that the mysterious letter she received and Subhi's choice to testify have brought them renewed hope and the possibility of freedom.

The Jackets

Key quotes

'The Jacket shakes his head and lets go of Eli, cuffing him hard across the ear so that Eli loses his balance and ends up on the dirt.' (p.59)

'They say it was Eli's fault. They say he started all the craziness ... They are saying he went for Beaver. That he fell. That Beaver tried to save him.' (p.208)

On a literal level, the Jackets are the security staff who work in the centre. However, as their management company and the government are omitted from the narrative, the Jackets also represent these groups as the enforcers of their policies. They check IDs, enforce curfews, serve contaminated food, and patrol with batons, dogs and beeper wands. Subhi tells us that some of the Jackets 'can be nice enough' (p.11) but as a group they are indifferent to the detainees' needs and suffering. Instances of rough handling, waking detainees to harass them and arbitrary reprimands suggest that some Jackets are actively hostile. By covering up Beaver's crime and making Eli a scapegoat for the riot, the Jackets are shown to be immoral and unmerciful.

Harvey

Key quote

'But Harvey loves me. He nods, to let me know that it's all right. That he understands. Then he is gone. And I never see Harvey again. Not ever.' (p.223)

Harvey is unlike the other guards. He is kind to the detainees and treats them humanely, often breaching protocols to do so – for example, calling people by their names rather than identification numbers. He is a father-figure to Subhi, showing him affection, bringing him gifts and trying to protect him during the riots. Harvey's silence after Eli's death and during the ensuing cover-up horrifies Subhi and puts him in the heart-wrenching position of having to betray Harvey in order to get justice for Eli. Harvey's silence is in part a result of him feeling indebted to Beaver for saving his life years before, raising questions about personal responsibility and obligation. He shows evidence of remorse, shame and regret in the days following Eli's death but continues to stay silent. His encouragement of Subhi as he is about to tell the truth to investigators reveals a willingness to accept the consequences of his actions, which paves the way for Subhi to forgive him. Harvey is a rounded, dynamic character, with flaws that reflect genuine human experiences and challenges, and his failure to act contradicts readers' expectations of him.

Beaver

Key quotes

'Eli says Beaver hates all of us because one time he almost got killed when a man in here turned crazy and grabbed a hammer. Beaver ended up losing his eye because of it ...' (p.31)

'... the way Beaver slapped one of the mums that time, right in front of everyone, and everyone just turned away, even Harvey.' (p.183)

It appears that Beaver is conducting a vendetta against detainees, having lost an eye in an earlier confrontation. He is a source of Subhi's nightmares and seems to intimidate the other guards, given no one ever challenges him for abusing his authority. The brutality of his assault and murder of Eli is enhanced by the obvious size difference between the two and the fact that Beaver strikes the fatal blow while Eli is beaten and defenceless. This symbolises the immense imbalance of power between detainees and immigration staff, while the ensuing cover-up alludes to a corrupt system. Beaver is the antagonist of the story and is a static character (that is, he does not change).

Other detainees

Key quotes

'There are only fourteen pairs of real shoes in this whole entire camp, even though there must be near about 900 pairs of feet.' (p.24)

'The man has only strong in his eyes, and I can see where he's used that string to stitch his own lips shut.' (p.142)

The detainees are in conflict with the guards and the institutions they embody. They are represented sympathetically as a united community with shared experiences of deprivation, trauma and fear. They are segregated into different compounds for families, single men, troublemakers, new arrivals and those needing protection or medical supervision. Characters such as Nasir, Fara and Remi illustrate a range of policies and procedures that exacerbate the detainees' suffering. Some other detainees call Subhi 'Aussie Boy' (p.113), emphasising the irony of Subhi having lived in Australia his whole life without having any rights as a resident or citizen.

Nasir is like a grandfather to Subhi, demonstrating how much the detainees need community. Nasir's characterisation positions readers to view his adverse security assessment and indefinite detention as unjust, particularly as his kindness, physical disability and senility make it difficult to believe he poses a threat.

Saleem, another detainee, represents the issue of people smugglers and the dangers people face coming to Australia by boat. He used 'every bit of money he could find' but was lied to about the safety of the boat and journey, which resulted in the deaths of his family (p.136). These stories work to humanise the controversial issue of boat arrivals.

The Shakespeare duck

Key quotes

'I tell the Shakespeare duck that I rescued from Harvey, and he looks me up and down with his little duck eyes and says that clearly I'm done for and could I please arrange for someone nice to take him when I'm dead.' (p.23)

'"It seems to me that you have a simple choice," the duck says. "Do nothing or tell what happened."' (p.210)

The Shakespeare duck is a toy brought into the centre by Harvey. (It is a real toy too – look it up online!) His parodic resemblance to the playwright William Shakespeare is humorous and his motto – '*To quack or not to quack*' (p.15) – hints at the novel's themes, in particular, those related to speaking up about injustice and voicelessness. Subhi is immediately attracted to the duck's plucky resolve when, being stomped on in the water, it 'keeps bobbing back up, smiling a little duck smile' (p.14). Subhi is the only one who appreciates the duck's worth and the only one who hears him, reflecting Subhi's desire to be seen.

The Shakespeare duck is a 'Wisecracking Sidekick', an archetype that appears as a hero's confidant, providing comic relief through witticism and jokes. These characters play a pivotal role in the hero's development and frequently offer a voice of reason. Other well-known examples include Sancho Panza in *Don Quixote* by Miguel de Cervantes, Genie in Disney's *Aladdin* and Mercutio in Shakespeare's *Romeo and Juliet*.

While the duck is endowed with a personality, thoughts and dialogue, he is essentially an extension of Subhi's character. Subhi's perception of having rescued the duck reflects his own desire to be rescued; like a security blanket, the duck provides comfort as Subhi's mother slips away. Taking ownership of the toy gives Subhi a sense of self, alleviating the loss of dignity, self-worth and autonomy caused by long-term deprivation and confinement. As an extension of his inner voice, the duck often challenges and contradicts Subhi, helping him wrestle with his fears and moral dilemmas.

THEMES, IDEAS & VALUES

Refugees and asylum seekers

The novel poses many questions to readers: Who deserves to come to Australia? Is detention ethical? Is it right to detain children? Who is complicit in the harms caused by mandatory detention – the government, facility management, ordinary citizens? How can we do better?

The refugee experience

Key quotes

'... we aren't wanted in this place, or in Burma, or in any other place ... we aren't wanted anywhere.' (p.110)

'Many would fear that they had been forgotten by a world that seemed deaf to the cries of those in need, a world in which hope is in short supply.' (p.224)

The novel illustrates many causes and consequences of forced displacement. Subhi's family are Rohingya and their people's persecution is directly addressed in Chapter Five. As stateless people, they have no right to citizenship anywhere in the world and so, unless another country grants them asylum, they have no chance of being afforded basic human rights. Fraillon includes a powerful detail about soldiers putting Subhi's sister and pregnant mother on a boat, telling them 'if they come back to Burma they'd be killed' (p.36). This renders the family completely blameless for their situation, which in turn represents their decade-long detention as a heartless response to their suffering.

The novel endorses humanitarian values and justifies the right to seek asylum. Refugee characters are conveyed sympathetically, including the boys who bully Subhi, as it is implied their behaviour is an outcome of detention (See 'Children in detention', p.52). Fraillon also endorses the need for asylum by representing detainees as vulnerable and traumatised through Maá's depression, references to self-harm and suicide, and the terror experienced by children seeing the guards in riot gear in Chapter Twenty-Eight. Furthermore, the novel promotes empathy for refugees by revealing the dangerous and gruelling journeys that preceded their arrival in Australia, such as Eli escaping in a crammed truck that caused his brother's death and Saleem's experiences with people smugglers and losing his family at sea. Both characters' suffering is compounded by family separation. Subhi tells us that being sent back home 'is the worst thing that can happen in here' (p.163). This raises the question: if that is worse than indefinite detention in inhumane conditions, how bad must home be?

Inhumane policies

Key quotes

'Here, we are the dead rats they leave out to stop other rats from coming.' (Queeny, p.110)

'Sometimes there's no doctor here for months, and when that happens, you just have to hope on not getting sick.' (p.135)

The novel alludes to numerous policies regarding refugees and asylum seekers, including mandatory detention; offshore processing; secrecy laws; and refusing settlement to, and using harsh detention conditions to deter, boat arrivals. These are represented as cold-hearted owing to their impact on detainees, who suffer mental illness, hopelessness, fear, confusion and disempowerment as a consequence. Taking into account the rights specified in the 1951 Refugee Convention, the representation of the detainees' suffering presents a scathing criticism of Australia's policies.

The novel paints a horrific picture of detention. Refugees are treated like prisoners, ironically living in conditions that are worse than those in Australian prisons. They are abused and demeaned, fed out-of-date and contaminated food that makes them sick, live in mouldy and rat-infested tents, use deficient sanitation facilities, and are not provided sufficient medical care, water, clothing, shoes, toiletries, toilet paper or sanitary products. Furthermore, the novel implies that the operators of the facility know conditions are unacceptable – they provide detainees with 'real eggs and real toast' when 'Guests' visit (p.85), suggesting a duplicitous attempt to conceal their human rights violations.

The novel encourages outrage at these dehumanising practices. Detainees are referred to by identification numbers, robbing them of their individuality and dignity. Strict rules prohibiting mobile phones, cameras and access to the media prevent detainees from reporting abuse and obtaining support. Chapter Thirteen describes characters being denied medicine, and the confiscation of Nasir's prosthetic leg and Fara's hearing aid appears irrational and cruel, and also in violation of the Declaration on the Rights of Disabled Persons. Nasir's adverse risk assessment seems unconscionable given his disability and his characterisation as kind and humble, and the transfer of children to adult compounds, resulting in a nine-year-old boy trying to 'bleed himself out on the fence', is outright shocking (p.58).

Tensions in the camp build gradually, so that by the time the Alpha men begin their protest we can understand the motivation behind drastic actions such as sewing their lips shut. Queeny's photograph of the protest is published by the media, but 'doesn't seem to do much' (p.151), rationalising the continued escalation of hostility so that the impending riot appears inevitable.

Key point

Several events in the novel are inspired by real events, many occurring at the Manus Island detention centre. These include human teeth being found in food, mass food poisoning and $30 000 worth of Freedom Foods muesli bars being rejected by management. Eli's death echoes the murder of Reza Berati, who was killed when guards hit him on the head with a piece of wood with a nail on the end of it and a large rock during a riot in 2014.

Children in detention

Key quotes

'Someday I'll be able to go to the toilet whenever I like and sit for as long as I like and use as much toilet paper as I like, just like Jimmie.' (p.115)

'... I don't know about things that soft. There isn't much soft in here.' (p.115)

One of the most compelling features of the novel is its representation of a child's perspective, which is intensified by Subhi never knowing life outside detention and being deprived of things that many would consider markers of a 'normal' childhood. Children in detention suffer from mental illness, nightmares and lack of nurturing. They are deprived of toys and play equipment, and resort to playing with rocks and racing lice. In contravention of international law, they are also denied an education, as demonstrated in Chapter Sixteen, which also describes Queeny teaching children to read and write. The need to take on adult responsibilities, and thus being forced to grow up too quickly, is also demonstrated when Queeny steps into a pseudo-parental role as Maá's mental health declines, and when Queeny and Eli participate in the protest. While many children in Australia might wish for game consoles, expensive sneakers or overseas holidays, Subhi wishes for ample supplies of toilet paper. When he, Queeny and Eli fantasise about being in charge of the centre, they do not dream about expensive toys but rather about good food, ample drinking water and 'hot-chocolate rain falling from the sky' (p.60).

Eli's murder at the hands of a guard epitomises the dangers children face in detention and plays on readers' emotions by going against everything most believe is right. While there is no evidence of children being murdered in Australian facilities, unnecessary deaths of children in detention have occurred here and around the world (Torre 2016; Roberts 2020), and children in many overseas camps are subjected to violence, human trafficking and other atrocities.

Attitudes to refugees

Key quotes

'Jimmie feels the howl in her throat turn from happy to sad at the unfairness of it all. How could people be so mean to each other when isn't everyone just the same anyway and why can't anyone work that out?' (p.103)

'... they put people into the Transit Centre and they all got beaten up and pissed on and told to go back to where they came from.' (Eli, p.139)

The novel challenges many attitudes prevalent in Australian society. Apathy is challenged through the empathetic representation of the detainees' suffering. The antipathy demonstrated by Beaver and some other guards is challenged by largely silencing these characters – their views are denied space in the novel – and representing them as cruel. Some of the myths perpetuating anti-refugee sentiments in the Australian public are debunked, such as the complaint of Jimmie's classmates that the detainees have 'good clothes and thousands of toys and books and computers and teachers and doctors' (p.43), and the notion that refugees should go 'back to where they came from' (p.163).

In contrast, the novel promotes empathy and compassion through the sympathetic representation of trauma; the positive qualities characters such as Subhi, Nasir, Queeny and Eli are endowed with; and the attitudes displayed by Jimmie and her family, for instance when Jimmie recalls her mother saying that detention is 'no way to treat people' (p.44). Jimmie's empathy and kindness make Subhi feel 'like someone is really seeing' him (p.126), and their relationship gives Subhi hope, purpose and courage. This conveys to readers that such attitudes are the antidote to injustice and are to be aspired to.

Key point

The criticisms of immigration policies and the attitudes represented in the novel are underpinned by a belief in human rights and the values of justice, equality, fairness, freedom, family, multiculturalism, egalitarianism, safety and security. It is useful to think about these when forming an interpretation and considering how your own values influence your response.

The power of stories

Key quotes

'… sometimes, in here, when people stop talking, and stop asking, and stop remembering, that's when they start to lose that piece of themselves.' (p.37)

'If we all sing together, our song can light up the dark.' (p.138; p.207)

Storytelling is a fundamental aspect of the human experience. Throughout history, we have shared stories for entertainment, education and connection. Stories take many forms, and mediums such as myth, art, music, dance and theatre have played a vital role in the formation and expression of identity for both past and present societies. Maá's 'Listen Now stories' (p.36) represent the cultural significance of stories in allowing people to sustain identity, teach history and bring joy. Subhi relies on them to connect with his culture and suffers when Maá is no longer able to share them. Likewise, repeated references to Maá, Jimmie's mother and Anka singing convey the nurturing and celebratory powers of song, while Eli's whale story symbolises the function of storytelling in forging human connections. Furthermore, Subhi's drawings are a creative outlet that give him purpose, preserve others' memories, and maintain hope and identity.

The transformative power of stories is evident when Maá's *taranas* change 'the heavy in the air' causing the detainees to 'keep that smiling and happy feel for days' (p.138) and when the Bone Sparrow story brings Jimmie and Subhi together. Jimmie's need to hear her mother's stories combines with Subhi's excitement at the sight of her book, as he has read everything there is to read in the centre, providing a catalyst for their relationship. Soon they begin to share other stories and, as the friendship deepens, both find the happiness and healing they so desperately need. This ability of stories and art to unite people is also evident when Subhi recalls 'Maá singing the *tarana* songs in Rohingya, and all of us joining in', including a guard who played along on his guitar (p.207). This suggests that stories and art can unite people, and that such a connection can transcend hierarchies and systemic divisions. Maá tells Subhi that 'if everyone would listen to the stories deep down inside the earth, we would hear the whisperings of everything there is to hear, and if everyone did that, then just maybe we wouldn't all get stuck so much' (p.47). The implication is that we have lost touch with our humanity and need to let go of the social constructs that divide us. Listening to each other's stories fosters empathy and compassion, which are essential if we are to tackle complex problems like injustice and prejudice.

Grief, loss and trauma

Key quotes

'Most days Jimmie can go the whole day without feeling that thirsting inside. But there is a lump, and a heaviness that never goes away.' (p.20)

'All I'm left with is an echoing kind of empty, and my stomach feels as though it has been kicked by a truck, and I get what Eli meant about his heart bleeding because mine is doing that right now.' (p.205)

The loss experienced by the detainees in the centre is protracted and immense. They have lost homes, loved ones, freedom, security, autonomy and just about every personal possession. As time passes in detention, detainees face the prospect of losing their identity and hope as well. Several references to self-harm and suicide demonstrate just how prevalent this suffering can be. Maá's story illustrates this downward spiral in a compelling way as readers learn what she used to be like and watch her continued decline through her son's eyes. Her illness results in an inability to care for her children, which is not uncommon in detention; this exacerbates Subhi and Queeny's loss and worsens an already traumatic situation. Likewise, the older boys who bully Subhi, and the men in Alpha who 'can be real mean to a kid' (p.58), are represented as having changed over time, suggesting they have been corrupted by the trauma of detention. Subhi experiences many forms of loss throughout the narrative, emphasising the injustice and horror of being a refugee child in an Australian immigration detention facility. Already suffering the trauma of losing his freedom and many aspects of his cultural identity, he learns his father has died and witnesses the brutal murder of his best friend.

The parallels between Subhi's and Jimmie's narratives remind readers that, while the trauma suffered by refugees might be vastly different from anything many Australians have experienced, at a fundamental level grief and loss are universal experiences. We are introduced to Jimmie in Chapter Three on the third anniversary of her mother's death. That Jimmie 'can't hear her mum's voice' (p.22) correlates with Subhi trying to hear his father's voice in the shell at the end of Chapter One, while the image of Jimmie's father howling in anguish echoes Maá's 'tired days' (p.2). Both Jimmie and Subhi are mourning a lost parent, and both cling to a living parent who is crippled by their own grief after the death of their spouse. As the plot progresses, Subhi and Jimmie's friendship becomes an antidote to their grief, reinforcing the value of social cohesion as we are reminded that relationships, connection and a sense of belonging are fundamental human needs.

Humour is represented as a coping tool and as having an important social function. Telling jokes helps Eli and Subhi maintain optimism and the impact of this is emphasised as the darkening tone of their interactions reflects the building tensions and hostility in the centre. The Shakespeare duck's wisecracks and witty retorts reflect Subhi's need for humour to lighten the weight of his difficult reality, and also help him work through some of his darker thoughts. Furthermore, Subhi and Jimmie find common ground through jokes. While Subhi does not always comprehend the context of Jimmie's jokes, their shared understanding of how jokes work and what it means to joke around with someone allows them to bridge the divide between their cultural backgrounds and personal circumstances.

Taking action

Key quotes

'*To quack or not to quack.*' (p.15)

'But then the newspaper people and their cameras were stopped from visiting …' (p.106)

'And everyone needs to know, to feel that pain tearing at them, even if just for a bit. Just so they know that once there lived a Limbo kid named Eli, and he had something important to do.' (p.213)

If 'quack' is a metonym for 'speak', then the Shakespeare duck's motto foreshadows the difficult choice Subhi is faced with, in the falling action section of the narrative: to tell the truth and get Harvey in trouble, or to protect Harvey and keep Eli's murder a secret. Subhi's decision to speak up at the end of the novel reveals a significant transformation of his character. Earlier challenges caused him to freeze, such as when the older boys made him kill the baby rat and when Beaver murdered Eli. While most readers would recognise that such a response is perfectly understandable given his age, Subhi's principles make him feel shame and regret for his inaction. These earlier events emphasise the significance of Subhi finding the courage to speak up, which, when juxtaposed with Harvey's failure to do the same, positions readers to accept the notion that everyone has responsibility to act against injustice.

Queeny's attempts to conceal her camera and the fact that journalists are banned from the centre suggest that laws and policies act to silence detainees, conceal the way in which they're treated and keep the public in the dark. Queeny's defiance of the draconian regulations and unchecked authority of the guards is an admirable act of courage for a child. However, the fact that none of the detainees' attempts to improve their living conditions seem to make much difference indicates the full extent of their oppression. Only after a child is violently murdered, triggering an investigation that allows Subhi to speak up and be heard, does change seem possible. It is ironic that Eli was the sole survivor of the truck journey that killed his brother, which Subhi believed was proof Eli 'had something important to do' (p.201), only to end up dying in such a barbaric and unjust manner. In a way, Eli is a sacrificial lamb, a blameless child who had to die so that others might survive. This irony highlights the terrible injustice of detention and appeals to the value of childhood innocence. Harvey's fall from grace emphasises how even people who care can be complicit in injustice. The representation of Harvey as a positive and likeable character, who appears principled when he swims against the tide to treat the detainees humanely, makes his inaction and silence shocking and disheartening. The resolution avoids a trite attempt at a happy ending in which all problems are neatly resolved, which would be unrealistic given that the issue is so complex and the problem ongoing. The impending trial gives us hope that change is possible, but the openness of the ending reminds readers that there is still a great deal that needs to happen to bring justice for refugees.

Regional disadvantage

Key quotes

'It's not like Jimmie is the only one not going to school.' (p.39)

'Now it's a fifty-minute drive to get a bottle of milk, meaning that more often than not Jimmie eats her cereal with water, or doesn't bother with breakfast at all.' (p.43)

Transience is common in the face of limited employment opportunities for unskilled workers in regional areas, and we see the impact of this in Jimmie's lack of friends due to moving house so frequently. Likewise, her inability to read suggests gaps in learning, presumably contributed to by numerous school changes. Jimmie's schooling is further disrupted by absenteeism due to her current school being an hour's drive away and the bus only coming past 'once a day' (p.39). The local town has been mostly shut down after the closure of the local mines, resulting in her father having to take a job 'working shifts, which took him away from home for days at a time' (p.41), signifying their geographical isolation. Due to this, Jimmie is often left alone and it appears the family has no access to help from the community. There is no doubt Jimmie's family members are doing their best and the neglect Jimmie experiences is represented as a tragic consequence of her mother's death and her socioeconomic and geographical circumstances, rather than the failings of her father. Jonah's tendency to go off drinking with his friends hints at the lack of educational and employment opportunities for youth in regional areas, and the depiction of their town as virtually abandoned, with empty houses and stores, suggests that economic problems in regional areas impact people's ability to forge and maintain communities.

Key point

The humanitarian values underpinning the themes related to refugees and asylum seekers also underpin Jimmie's characterisation as representative of regional disadvantage. The parallels between Jimmie and Subhi's adversity remind us that disadvantage is widespread, and that marginalisation can affect anyone, regardless of citizenship status. However, there are notable disparities between Jimmie's and Subhi's levels of disadvantage. While Jimmie's town is destitute and she frequently goes without breakfast and has difficulty getting to school, the family have access to basic necessities and their modest home is comfortable and safe. This emphasises the direness of the conditions that Subhi must live with, as even Jimmie's disadvantaged circumstances are shown to be far superior to his.

DIFFERENT INTERPRETATIONS

Different interpretations arise from different responses to a text. Over time, a text will evoke a wide range of responses from its readers, who may come from various social or cultural groups and live in very different places and historical periods. Responses by critics and reviewers can be published in newspapers, journals and books, both online and in print. They can also be expressed in discussions among readers in the media, classrooms, book groups and so on.

While there is no single correct reading or interpretation of a text, it is important to understand that an interpretation is more than a personal opinion – it is the justification of a point of view on the text. To present an interpretation of a text based on your point of view, you must use a logical argument and support it with relevant evidence from the text.

The critics' viewpoints

Overwhelmingly, *The Bone Sparrow* has received glowing reviews and accolades since it was published. Having won and been shortlisted for several prestigious awards, Fraillon has been praised for her ability to compose a poignant children's book that humanises the experience of refugees.

Fraillon won the 2017 Amnesty CILIP Honour, a prize awarded to a text shortlisted for prestigious British literary award the Carnegie Medal, which promotes justice and human rights. In his blog post about the novel, judge Bali Rai called it 'a wonderfully written and plotted tale' that is 'a wonderful instrument for empathy, promoting better understanding of the human lives behind sensationalist and horrific headlines' (Rai 2017). He makes particular mention of Fraillon's ability to balance confronting content with a message of hope.

Judges for Australia's 2017 Prime Minister's Literary Awards, for which *The Bone Sparrow* was shortlisted, commended Fraillon's masterful use of imagery, language and motif in provoking thought and emotional resonance. Remarking on the novel's impact, they wrote:

> Set against the harshness and brutality of life in the detention centre, *The Bone Sparrow* celebrates human courage, spirit and imagination; the power of story, especially in our understanding of self; the importance of friendship; and our right to freedom. (DITRDC 2017)

Two interpretations

Interpretation 1: *The Bone Sparrow* is a harrowing story about Australia's failure as a nation to live up to its own values.

The Bone Sparrow paints a grim picture of Australia as a nation plagued by moral and political corruption. The introduction of the Shakespeare duck in Chapter Two hints at this theme. The duck's motto, '*To quack or not to quack*' (p.15), is a twist on the famous line 'to be or not to be' from Shakespeare's *Hamlet*, a play that explores the central theme of a nation decaying due to moral and political corruption.

The issue of how to handle refugees and asylum seekers has been highly politicised in Australia since the 1990s, with many politicians scaremongering to justify tough policies, and appealing to public fear during elections. Examples include former prime minister John Howard's famously emphatic declaration that 'we will decide who comes to this country and the circumstances in which they come' (Howard 2001), former prime minister Tony Abbott's repeated references to a need to 'stop the boats' (Joseph 2015), and former immigration minister Peter Dutton's claim that refugees would 'take Australian jobs' (Yaxley 2016). These attitudes are challenged in *The Bone Sparrow*, which highlights the human impact of such rhetoric. The choice of a nine-year-old protagonist appeals to readers' sympathies to make the policies seem especially brutal. Furthermore, by exposing readers to human suffering in cruel conditions, Fraillon suggests that those who legislate and enforce Australia's immigration detention policies are guilty of a grievous disregard for decency and human rights.

Fraillon's insinuation of moral corruption at the government level is strengthened by the exclusion of politicians or bureaucrats from the list of characters. This absence reminds readers that the decision-makers rarely have to face the people affected by their policies. The suggestion that refugees are pawns in a political game is reinforced by Queeny's assertion that the detainees are 'the dead rats they leave out to stop other rats from coming' (p.110). The conditions in the camp not only breach multiple international laws, but also contravene the government's own claims about detention management. The Australian Border Force website states:

> We treat all people in detention with respect, dignity and fairness. While in an immigration detention facility, we provide appropriate food, medical, recreational and other support services, including mental health services. (ABF 2019)

Yet, a multitude of details in the novel refute this assertion. There are 'food shortages' (p.4) in Chapter One and a mass case of food poisoning in Chapter Eighteen. Maá is never offered any psychological treatment, children play with rocks, and the provision of basic toiletries, amenities and clothing is severely inadequate. Again, this suggests there is moral corruption at the highest level of Australian society, either due to negligence, because the government does not know what is happening in its facilities, or due to blatant deception, with the government attempting to conceal abuses of detainees.

Several events in the novel suggest that those operating the centre are apathetic and negligent. The acts of feeding people 'mush' contaminated with 'flies or worms' (p.4), transferring children to adult compounds, and treating detainees with casual cruelty suggest that facility staff and, by association, the politicians and citizens who support mandatory detention, do not care about the detainees' suffering. When Queeny challenges Eli's transfer to Alpha by pointing out that Eli is only a child, the guard replies that paperwork 'doesn't lie', suggesting contempt for truth and fairness (p.58). Such practices conflict with democratic values. Australians generally expect authorities to behave ethically, laws to be fair and equitable, and the government to be honest and transparent. Thus, when Subhi says 'writing does lie. It lies all the time' (p.58), readers are positioned to question the ethical validity of legislation concerning asylum seekers in Australia and feel outraged by the government's duplicity and hypocrisy.

The detention and treatment of children, in particular, is in stark contrast to Australian values, in which the innocence and rights of children are considered paramount. Yet, Subhi and the other children are living in deplorable conditions and denied schooling because it is 'too expensive' (p.109). *The Forgotten Children* report found that detention causes significant harm to children's development and their physical and mental health (AHRC 2014). We see evidence of this in references to children 'whumping' their heads on the ground (p.160) and the nine-year-old boy who attempted suicide by trying 'to bleed himself out on the fence' (p.58). Queeny tells Subhi she thinks the older boys who bully him and torture rats used to be like him, but have 'been here too long' (p.65). This suggests they have been corrupted, and that this corruption is a consequence of detention that could happen to Subhi as well.

The novel's criticisms are not exclusively directed at the government. The Jackets are Australian citizens who willingly disregard human welfare. Likewise, Jimmie's peers saying 'how lucky those people were in the Centre' (p.43) and Queeny's claim that the centre is 'just one big cage of invisible people who no one believes are even real' (p.126) reflect widespread apathy and ignorance in Australian society. When Harvey 'follows Beaver' and 'walks away' (p.199) from Eli's lifeless body, his actions defy the principles he previously appeared to have held. This is representative of Australians turning a blind eye to the suffering of people in detention, suggesting that the Australian public is complicit in the injustices committed by the government and, therefore, that moral corruption plagues Australia at every level.

Despite fairness, egalitarianism and freedom being touted as dominant Australian values, the nation has a history of ethnocentricity and segregation. Colonisation had a devastating impact on Australia's First Nations peoples, who have been subjected to numerous discriminatory and oppressive laws and practices. Likewise, immigration laws supporting the White Australia policy, such as the *Immigration Restriction Act 1901*, were xenophobic. Hence, it could be argued that current refugee legislation, and ignorance about and apathy towards asylum seekers and refugees among the broader public, is consistent with a history of marginalisation and institutionalised racism. Even today, despite a growing emphasis on multiculturalism and diversity, First Nations peoples and other ethnic minorities still face disadvantage, discrimination and hostility, suggesting that treating asylum seekers like 'rats' (p.110) is an extension of a much bigger systemic problem – that moral decay is at the heart of a nation that does not practice what it preaches.

Interpretation 2: *The Bone Sparrow* is a hopeful text that conveys how community, friendship and kindness can improve even the most difficult of situations.

The Bone Sparrow promotes the idea that simple acts of kindness can make a big difference. Subhi's life is one of misery and deprivation, yet he manages to sustain a kind spirit that improves his own life and the lives of others. When 'the oldies' ask him 'to draw them things' (p.157), he does, in part because he needs their stories, but also because it makes them 'their very own blanket to wrap themselves up in' (p.158), showing that just a little effort can bring others comfort. Subhi understands that when people lose their memories 'they start to lose that piece of themselves', which can make 'their brains start to mush' (p.37). As the older detainees struggle with senility and memory loss, Subhi's simple kindness makes a significant difference to their wellbeing.

When Jimmie returns to visit Subhi in Chapter Ten, it is because she wants him to read her mother's stories to her. However, when she arrives, she does not immediately demand that he read to her. She asks how long he has been in detention and about his family, showing a sincere interest in him as a person. On her next visit, she brings the Thermos of hot chocolate. She has no way of knowing that Subhi has never tasted hot chocolate and thus the intense pleasure it will bring him, but this simple act of consideration shows her generosity. As she gets to know Subhi better, she comes to understand more about the deprivation he suffers. Taking photographs to 'show him everything he has to look forward to' is a benevolent act that demonstrates goodwill towards him (p.104). When she sees Queeny's photograph of the protestors in the newspaper in Chapter Twenty, she is upset and confused about the inhumanity that Subhi and the other detainees suffer. In response she brings Subhi a feast (p.148). While this cannot resolve the injustice of detention, it shows Jimmie's willingness to go out of her way to bring Subhi pleasure. Her generosity results in Subhi experiencing 'one of the best things' in his life (p.149), which gives him a 'warm and full' sensation that is still there the next morning (p.153).

Other characters also demonstrate a willingness to do good for others. Harvey comes to work early with the paddling pool to offer the children a reprieve from the heat and the monotony of their lives. The impact of this is clear when Subhi puts his head under the water and 'the whole world stops' (p.16). Similarly, Eli's ability to make 'everything all right' is a result of his love manifested through kind acts (p.68). He gives Subhi shoes and a muesli bar, items he could have kept for himself, and he stopped the older boys from trapping rats, despite not caring about them himself, because he saw Subhi's face when he 'heard them squeal' (p.66). Queeny's act of leaving Ba's treasures for 'five seasons' (p.6) shows a prolonged act of consideration and selflessness. Though it is of no benefit to her, it preserves Subhi's innocence and hope by nurturing his belief in the Night Sea and his connection to the father he has never met.

QUESTIONS & ANSWERS

This section focuses on your own analytical writing on the text, and gives you strategies for producing high-quality responses in your coursework and exam essays.

Essay writing – an overview

An essay on a literary work is a formal and serious piece of writing that presents your point of view on the text, usually in response to a given topic. Your 'point of view' in an essay is your interpretation of the meaning of the text's language, structure, characters, situations and events, supported by detailed analysis of textual evidence.

Analyse – don't summarise

In your essays it is important to avoid simply summarising what happens in a text.

- A **summary** is a description or paraphrase (retelling in different words) of the characters and events. For example: 'Macbeth has a horrifying vision of a dagger dripping with blood before he goes to murder King Duncan.'
- An **analysis** is an explanation of the real meaning or significance that lies 'beneath' the text's words (and images, for a film). For example: 'Macbeth's vision of a bloody dagger shows how deeply uneasy he is about the violent act he is contemplating, and conveys his sense that supernatural forces are impelling him to act.'

A limited amount of summary is sometimes necessary to let your reader know which part of the text you wish to discuss. However, always keep this to a minimum and follow it immediately with your analysis of what this part of the text is really telling us.

Plan your essay

Carefully plan your essay so that you have a clear idea of what you are going to say. The plan ensures that your ideas flow logically, that your argument remains consistent and that you stay on the topic. An essay plan should be a list of **brief dot points** covering no more than half a page.

- Include your central argument or main contention – a concise statement of your overall response to the topic.
- Write three or four dot points for each paragraph, indicating the main idea and evidence/examples from the text. Note that in your essay you will need to *expand* on these points and *analyse* the evidence.

Structure your essay

An essay is a complete, self-contained piece of writing. It has a clear beginning (the introduction), middle (several body paragraphs) and end (the last paragraph or conclusion). It must also have a central argument that runs throughout, linking each paragraph to form a coherent whole. See examples of introductions and conclusions in the 'Analysing a sample topic' and 'Sample answer' sections.

The introduction establishes your overall response to the topic. It includes your main contention and outlines the main evidence you will refer to in the course of the essay. Write your introduction *after* you have done a plan and *before* you write the rest of the essay.

The body paragraphs argue your case – they present evidence from the text and explain how this evidence supports your argument. Each body paragraph needs:

- a strong **topic sentence** (usually the first sentence) that states the main point being made in the paragraph
- **evidence** from the text, including some brief quotations
- **analysis** of the textual evidence, with **explanation** of its significance and how it supports your argument
- **links back to the topic** in one or more statements, usually towards the end of the paragraph.

Connect the body paragraphs so that your discussion flows smoothly. Use some linking words and phrases such as 'similarly' and 'on the other hand', though don't start every paragraph like this. Another strategy is to use a significant word from the last sentence of one paragraph in the first sentence of the next.

Use key terms from the topic – or synonyms for them – throughout, so the relevance of your discussion to the topic is always clear.

The conclusion ties everything together and finishes the essay. It includes strong statements that emphasise your central argument and provide a clear response to the topic.

Avoid simply restating the points made earlier in the essay – this will end on a very flat note and imply that you have run out of ideas and vocabulary. The conclusion should be a logical extension of what you have written, not just a repetition or summary of it. Writing an effective conclusion can be a challenge. Try using these tips:

- Start by linking back to the final sentence of the second-last paragraph, rather than leaping to your main contention straight away – this helps your writing to flow.
- Use synonyms and expressions with equivalent meanings to vary your vocabulary. This allows you to reinforce your line of argument without being repetitive.
- When planning your essay, think of one or two broad statements or observations about the text's wider meaning. These should be related to the topic and your overall argument. Keep them for the conclusion, since they will give you something 'new' to say but still follow logically from your discussion. The introduction will be focused on the topic, but the conclusion can present a wider view of the text.

Essay topics

1. 'The Night Sea is central to the themes of *The Bone Sparrow*.' Discuss.
2. "Not ever can always change."
   Does the novel endorse Maá's view?
3. 'Harvey's silence after Eli's death is an act of cowardice.'
   Do you agree?
4. 'Subhi is not the only hero in *The Bone Sparrow*.'
   Do you agree?
5. "And now it's like those damn sparrows are everywhere."
   Discuss the role of birds in the novel.
6. "This is a tale from long, long ago."
   Discuss how Oto and Anka's story enhances the themes of the novel.
7. 'To evoke change, fiction must make us look at ourselves.'
   Discuss how this relates to *The Bone Sparrow*.
8. "I'm sick of being a dead rat."
   Discuss the role of Queeny's perspective in representing immigration detention in Australia.
9. 'Subhi's voice is the voice of all refugees.' Discuss.
10. 'The riot was the inevitable outcome of a series of avoidable events.'
    To what extent do you agree?

Vocabulary for writing on *The Bone Sparrow*

Allusion: an indirect or passing reference to fictional and real people, events or ideas.

Archetype: a commonly used type of character or situation found in many texts.

Circularity: a structural feature in which a story starts and finishes in the same place, literally or metaphorically.

Comic relief: a humorous character, scene or technique used to relieve tension.

Duality: the state of being divided into two opposing parts.

Egalitarianism: the belief in equal rights and opportunities for all.

Empathy: the ability to understand someone else's experiences or feelings.

Ethical: in accordance with moral principles.

Everyman Hero: an archetypal hero who possesses universal, ordinary qualities.

Humanitarian: related to human rights and welfare.

Ideology: a system of beliefs, attitudes and assumptions.

Idiolect: an individual's unique speech patterns.

Imagery: descriptive details used to evoke sensory experiences.

International law: rules based on a legally enforceable treaty, declaration or convention agreed upon by multiple nations.

Juxtaposition: the placement of contrasting elements side by side to highlight their differences.

Motif: a recurring phrase, image or idea with thematic significance.

Multiculturalism: the acceptance and celebration of multiple ethnic and cultural groups within a society.

Oppression: the denial of rights or freedom to a particular group by those in power.

Parallel point of view: the use of alternating narrators.

Persecution: systematic harassment, oppression or mistreatment.

Prejudice: negative and unfair or discriminatory judgement.

Representation: the portrayal of a group, person, idea, event or issue through specific details and textual features.

Segregation: the isolation of minorities from the dominant social group.

Symbolism: a word or image that represents an idea or theme.

Synecdoche: a figure of speech in which a part of something represents the whole.

Trauma: psychological injury resulting from deeply distressing experiences.

Unreliable narrator: a narrator whose perception is flawed, limited or not credible due to naivety, deception or delusion.

Analysing a sample topic

"This is a tale from long, long ago."
Discuss how Oto and Anka's story enhances the themes of the novel.

This topic requires you to consider the meaning of the Bone Sparrow story and how it relates to the themes of the novel. Inherent in this are the concepts of plot, characterisation and structure, including the story-within-a-story device, motifs and parallels. You might consider:

- the idea of cheating fate and Oto's perception of a 'charmed life'
- Anka's love song and how this relates to Jimmie's and Subhi's mothers
- the idea of all people being on a journey to peace
- Anka's inability to see
- parallels between Subhi's and Oto's families
- the mythic style of the story enhancing its function as an allegory
- the bird motif (Anka born of an egg, the Bone Sparrow)
- the Bone Sparrow necklace featuring prominently in both plots
- references to displacement and family separation
- Subhi's version of the end of Iliya's story.

Whatever features and ideas you discuss, you must explain *how* examples from Oto and Anka's story *enhance* themes. Make explicit links to other parts of the novel, and focus on how these parallels communicate ideas about refugees, inhumane policies, grief, loss, trauma and the power of stories.

Sample introduction

> Harmony and stability are essential for a safe, happy life and yet, throughout history, humanity has been plagued by war, social conflict and natural disasters. On a personal level, everyone experiences loss and grief at some point, making the quest for peace a constant and capricious journey. These ideas are at the heart of *The Bone Sparrow*, a novel in which characters endure conflict and the pain of family detachment. Oto and Anka's tale, a story within a story that allegorises the search for peace, presents many parallels to both Subhi's and Jimmie's lives. These parallels enhance the themes of refugee rights and human suffering, conveying that, in one way or another, all people are on a journey to find peace.

Body paragraph 1

- Oto and Anka are symbols for all displaced people.
- Examples include the myth-like opening that removes political context (p.78); the soldiers' invasion (p.117) that mirrors Subhi's family's suffering (p.36); and Subhi's realisation that they are all on the same journey to peace (p.209).
- Oto and Anka's story emphasises universal experiences of displacement, and likens the search for asylum to a search for peace.

Body paragraph 2

- Parallels between the families of Oto and Anka and of Subhi emphasise the suffering caused by family separation.
- Examples include Oto's journey to reunite with Anka (pp.117–18, pp.131–3, pp.177–8); Subhi's bond with his absent father when hearing his voice in a shell (p.8); Oto and Anka's reunion giving Subhi hope (p.178); and Subhi reconnecting with Queeny and Maá (pp.214–17, pp.225–8).
- Oto's literal journey to reunify his family mirrors Subhi's metaphorical journey to reconnect with his, bringing them both peace.

Body paragraph 3

- The Bone Sparrow necklace is a symbol of luck and protection, emphasising the need for safety.
- Examples include Jimmie's belief that the necklace protects her family (p.76); the fact that the necklace reunites Oto with Anka and he gives it to his son for protection (p.178); and Jimmie no longer needing the necklace once her father begins working closer to home, and so passing it on to Subhi (p.219).
- Parallels between the Bone Sparrow's role across both stories emphasise the interrelationship between family, safety and protection; Jimmie and Subhi find peace in reading Oto and Anka's story and knowing that they, too, can cheat fate.

Sample conclusion

Despite their vastly different backgrounds, Jimmie, Subhi, Oto and Anka desire the same thing: to feel safe and connected to family. This suggests that all humans are fundamentally alike, and that, regardless of appearance, language and culture, people suffer when their lives and families are disrupted or threatened. Oto and Anka's story parallels Jimmie's and Subhi's in ways that suggest that at the heart of the refugee experience is the innate human need to feel safe. Thus, *The Bone Sparrow* positions readers to understand that, while some journeys are more treacherous and controversial than others, we are all on the same journey: to find a way to cheat fate and live in peace.

SAMPLE ANSWER

'Harvey's silence after Eli's death is an act of cowardice.' Do you agree?

Zana Fraillon's novel *The Bone Sparrow* portrays immigration detention as an inhumane and oppressive enterprise, highlighted through the acute power imbalance between guards and detainees. The juxtaposition of two guards, Harvey and Beaver, is central to this. Harvey's benevolence contrasts with Beaver's cruelty to emphasise the dehumanisation experienced by detainees. However, when Beaver kills Eli, Harvey's refusal to speak up makes him complicit in a conspiracy to cover up criminal misconduct and protect a murderer. Harvey maintaining this silence reveals a weakness of character, as he fails to do what he knows is right. His silence also betrays innocent people and amounts to siding with a corrupt institution against victims fighting for justice and freedom. Thus, Harvey's refusal to speak up after Eli's murder is not merely an act of cowardice but also one of hostility.

Harvey's silence after Eli's death is not crisis-induced panic. Rather, it follows a pattern of weakness that becomes hostile. Early in the novel Subhi recounts Eli calling Harvey 'spineless', claiming he lets Beaver get away with things 'he wouldn't stand for' with other guards because he owes Beaver his life. As Beaver lost an eye and almost died while protecting Harvey from a violent detainee, we can infer that Harvey refuses 'to ever say anything bad against Beaver' because he feels indebted and possibly guilty. When Eli blames Harvey for Beaver assaulting Subhi, Harvey 'walks away' in silence, and his lack of protest implies an admission of guilt. Despite this, Harvey continues to knowingly enable Beaver with his silence, and when this leads to Eli's murder, Harvey still 'doesn't say anything'. This pattern suggests a calculated decision never to oppose Beaver, and, while Harvey's complicity once contributed only to the perpetuation of minor injustices, his silence following Eli's death protects a murderer. Not speaking up against Beaver's abuse is cowardly, but Harvey's commitment to acknowledging his debt to Beaver in the circumstances of Eli's murder is also a cruel betrayal of the detainees because it further empowers their oppressors.

Supporting this cover-up requires Harvey to betray his principles and reinforces the antagonistic division between detainees and guards. Harvey is initially portrayed as having strong morals and humanitarian values, evident in his affection for Subhi, refusal to use people's identification numbers 'even when he's supposed to', and attempt to alleviate the heat by bringing in the plastic pool for the children. However, Eli's murder brings the camp's hostilities to a crisis point, forcing Harvey to demonstrate which side he is on. Given the Australian context and the patriarchal culture implied by the behaviour of the guards, who 'play cards and drink' and exert dominance by 'cuffing' detainees across the ear, mateship would be a sacred and unquestionable virtue among centre personnel. Repetition of 'they say' and 'they are saying' in Subhi's recount of the cover-up conveys solidarity among the guards, while the fact that 'Harvey doesn't say' implies his reluctance to betray his colleagues, despite having previously distanced himself from them, calling them 'useless as teats on a bull'. That they deserve his loyalty more than the people he cares about suggests affection is valued less than commitment to the brotherhood. Thus, Harvey's silence reinforces a division between fellow countrymen and unwelcome outsiders, declaring the detainees to be his enemy and Eli's murder to be the battleline over which he combats them.

By siding with the guards Harvey also launches a cowardly attack on Subhi. His silence during the cover-up is a metaphoric blow to Subhi's heart that 'won't stop bleeding' – a description that likens the betrayal to a fatal and painful injury. When Subhi is about to reveal everything to investigators, Harvey 'nods' at him, indicating he knows that Subhi is doing the right thing by telling the 'story that has to be told'. At this point his silence serves no purpose; thus, he could speak up and alleviate Subhi from the burden of betraying him. Choosing silence again shows his willingness to let a child carry the responsibility of standing up to a dangerous man and a powerful institution. The 'sad' in his eyes and his 'single tear' indicate regret that only emphasises his weakness. Putting Subhi in this position is both cowardly and aggressive because it is a hurtful and treacherous act that forces a child to carry the burden of a man's wrongdoings, simply because the man lacks the courage to admit his own faults and failings.

While Harvey initially appears to be a kind and compassionate man who cares for Subhi and the other detainees, when given the opportunity to truly prove his worth, he betrays the people he cares about. Harvey's silence seems to be driven by self-interest and a misguided belief in the virtue of mateship, resulting in his acquiescence to the pressures of the 'boys' club' in which he works. The damage this does – breaking Subhi's heart and burdening him with the responsibility of seeking justice and standing up to corruption – proves that, while sometimes actions speak louder than words, silence can be deafening.

REFERENCES & READING

Text

Fraillon, Z 2016, *The Bone Sparrow*, Lothian, Australia.

References

ABF (Australian Border Force) 2019, *Immigration Detention in Australia*, ABF, https://www.abf.gov.au/about-us/what-we-do/border-protection/immigration-detention/detention-management

AHRC (Australian Human Rights Commission) 2013, *Tell Me About: Refugees with Adverse Security Assessments*, AHRC, https://humanrights.gov.au/our-work/asylum-seekers-and-refugees/publications/tell-me-about-refugees-adverse-security

—— 2014, *The Forgotten Children: National Inquiry into Children in Immigration Detention 2014*, AHRC, https://humanrights.gov.au/our-work/asylum-seekers-and-refugees/publications/forgotten-children-national-inquiry-children

Andrew & Renata Kaldor Centre for International Refugee Law 2019, *Immigration Detention in Australia*, University of New South Wales, https://www.kaldorcentre.unsw.edu.au/publication/immigration-detention-australia

BBC (British Broadcasting Corporation) 2020, 'Myanmar Rohingya: World court orders prevention of genocide', BBC News, 23 January, https://www.bbc.com/news/world-asia-51221029

Blakemore, E 2019, 'Who are the Rohingya people?', *National Geographic*, 9 February, https://www.nationalgeographic.com/culture/article/rohingya-people

DHA (Department of Home Affairs) 2021, *Australian Values*, DHA, https://www.homeaffairs.gov.au/about-us/our-portfolios/social-cohesion/australian-values

DITRDC (Department of Infrastructure, Transport, Regional Development and Communications) 2017, *The Bone Sparrow*, DITRDC, https://www.arts.gov.au/pm-literary-awards/current-awards/bone-sparrow

Fiske, L 2016, *Human Rights, Refugee Protest and Immigration Detention*. Palgrave Macmillan, London.

Fraillon, Z n.d., *Zana Fraillon,* https://www.zanafraillon.com

Fraillon, Z 2016, 'Zana Fraillon on writing about refugee children: Their resilience keeps hope alive', *The Guardian*, 16 November, https://www.theguardian.com/books/booksblog/2016/nov/15/zana-fraillon-writing-about-refugee-children-the-bone-sparrow-guardian-childrens-fiction-award

Howard, J 2001, *2001 John Howard*, Australian Federal Election Speeches, https://electionspeeches.moadoph.gov.au/speeches/2001-john-howard

JSCAIDN (Joint Select Committee on Australia's Immigration Detention Network) 2012, 'Chapter 5: The impact of detention', Final Report, Parliament of Australia, https://www.aph.gov.au/Parliamentary_Business/Committees/Joint/Former_Committees/immigrationdetention/report/c05

Joseph, S 2015, 'Operation Sovereign Borders, offshore detention and the "drownings argument" ', *The Conversation*, 24 July, https://theconversation.com/operation-sovereign-borders-offshore-detention-and-the-drownings-argument-45095

Karlson, E 2016, 'Refugee resettlement to Australia: what are the facts?', Parliament of Australia, https://www.aph.gov.au/About_Parliament/Parliamentary_Departments/Parliamentary_Library/pubs/rp/rp1617/refugeeresettlement

LCA (Law Council of Australia) 2014, *Law Council of Australia Asylum Seeker Policy*, LCA, https://www.lawcouncil.asn.au/policy-agenda/human-rights/immigration-detention-and-asylum-seekers

Murray, K, Davidson, G and Schweitzer, R 2008, *Psychological Wellbeing of Refugees Resettling in Australia*, Australian Psychological Society, https://www.psychology.org.au/About-Us/What-we-do/advocacy/Position-Papers-Discussion-Papers-and-Reviews/Psychological-wellbeing-refugees-resettling-Aus

OHCHR (Office of the High Commissioner for Human Rights) 2012, *Universal Declaration of Human Rights*, Stand Up for Human Rights, https://www.standup4humanrights.org/en/article.html

Rai, B 2017, 'Author Bali Rai on new Amnesty CILIP Honour winner "The Bone Sparrow"', Amnesty International UK, 19 June, https://www.amnesty.org.uk/blogs/stories-rights/author-bali-rai-new-amnesty-cilip-honour-winner-bone-sparrow

RCOA (Refugee Council of Australia) 2021, *Statistics on people in detention in Australia*, RCOA, https://www.refugeecouncil.org.au/detention-australia-statistics/5/

Roberts, W 2020, 'Deaths of migrant children in US custody could have been averted', *Al Jazeera*, 15 July, https://www.aljazeera.com/news/2020/7/15/deaths-of-migrant-children-in-us-custody-could-have-been-averted

Rohingya Cultural Centre 2020, *History of the Rohingya*, Rohingya Cultural Centre, https://rccchicago.org/history/

Senate Community Affairs References Committee 2004, 'Chapter 14 - Rural and regional communities', *A hand up not a hand out: Renewing the fight against poverty*, Parliament of Australia, https://www.aph.gov.au/parliamentary_business/committees/senate/community_affairs/completed_inquiries/2002-04/poverty/report/c14

Shakespeare, W 2008, *Hamlet*, Floating Press, New Zealand.

Tlozek, E 2016, 'Reza Barati death: Two men jailed over 2014 murder of asylum seeker at Manus Island detention centre', ABC News, 19 April, https://www.abc.net.au/news/2016-04-19/reza-barati-death-two-men-sentenced-to-10-years-over-murder/7338928

Torre, G 2016, 'Exclusive: Mystery surrounds deaths in immigration detention as answers are delayed or denied', *Perth Now*, 2 August, https://www.perthnow.com.au/community-news/eastern-reporter/exclusive-mystery-surrounds-deaths-in-immigration-detention-as-answers-are-delayed-or-denied-c-779626

UNHCR (United Nations High Commissioner for Refugees) 2017, *Global Trends – Forced Displacement in 2016*, UNHCR, https://www.unhcr.org/globaltrends2016/

United States Holocaust Memorial Museum 2020, *Burma's Path to Genocide*, United States Holocaust Memorial Museum, https://exhibitions.ushmm.org/burmas-path-to-genocide/timeline

Yaxley, L 2016, 'Dutton accused of scare campaign over comments that more refugees would take Australian jobs', [video] ABC News, 18 May, https://www.abc.net.au/radio/programs/am/dutton-accused-of-scare-campaign-over-comments/7424266

Young, K 2017, 'Who are the Rohingya and what is happening in Myanmar?' Amnesty International Australia, 26 September, https://www.amnesty.org.au/who-are-the-rohingya-refugees/

Further reading

Berti, B & Borgman, E 2016, 'What does it mean to be a refugee?', [video], TED-Ed, YouTube, 17 June, https://www.youtube.com/watch?v=25bwiSikRsI

Morrison, S 2014, 'Scott Morrison: asylum seekers must go home or face "a very, very long time" in detention', [video] *The Guardian*, 25 June, https://www.theguardian.com/world/video/2014/jun/25/scott-morrisons-urges-asylum-seekers-to-return

RCOA 2020, *Timeline of refugees and Australia*, RCOA, https://www.refugeecouncil.org.au/timeline

UNHCR n.d., *The 1951 Refugee Convention*, UNHCR, https://www.unhcr.org/en-au/1951-refugee-convention.html